THE INCREDIBLE MISSION
OF FATHER BENOÎT

The Incredible Mission of Father Benoît

FERNANDE LEBOUCHER
TRANSLATED BY J. F. BERNARD

WILLIAM KIMBER
LONDON

First Published in Great Britain in 1970 by
WILLIAM KIMBER & CO. LIMITED
6 Queen Anne's Gate, London, S.W.1.

Printed in Great Britain by
W & J Mackay & Co Ltd, Chatham

Contents

FOREWORD   7

I: FRANCE
  1   The Beginnings: Marseilles   11
  2   The Background   41
  3   The Rescue   64

II: ITALY
  1   June 1943–September 1943:
      The Tragedy of Nice   107
  2   September 1943–June 1944: Rome   136

  EPILOGUE   190

Foreword

The author, in gathering material for this book, has relied upon two principal sources. The first is the notes, letters, and records she collected during World War II, at a time when she was an active participant in many of the events described. The second is memory—her own, and that of Father Marie-Benoît, OFM Cap. To the first source is due the general framework of the book and the direction that it has taken. To the second are due the details of background, conversations, dialogues, and incidents. If memory, at a distance of nearly a quarter of a century, has occasionally failed—if a name has been recalled incorrectly, or not at all; if a date or place has been inaccurately cited—then the author asks the reader's kind indulgence for these sins both of omission and commission. The human memory, after all, is the most fallible record of human achievement.

FERNANDE LEBOUCHER

I
France

I

Marseilles: The Beginning

THE rue Croix-de-Regnier in Marseilles is a
street indistinguishable from dozens of others
like it. There are old buildings greyed by the passage of
time to that patina common enough in Europe; there
are a few shops, a few bistros, a few street vendors.
Among these pedestrian surroundings stands the Capuchin convent of Marseilles. Its inhabitants, brown-
clad and bearded monks, shod even on the coldest days
only in sandals, give to the street its only claim to the
extraordinary. Making their way in and out of number
51, their anachronistic habits flapping in the wind, they
seem an apparition out of the reign of some Valois king.

Today, in the late 1960s, the convent is a place of
study, of contemplation, of tranquillity. It was not,
however, always so. Early in the fifth decade of this
century, number 51 rue Croix-de-Regnier, even while
it housed young friars studying for the priesthood and
older friars whose chief delight lay in the subtleties of
theology, was a centre of illegal activity. Criminal acts
were committed there: forgeries, the concealment of

persons hunted by the police, the collection of money for illegal purposes. Because of these activities, the monks of that time had been in constant danger of arrest; and the convent itself was more than once in imminent danger of being raided by the police. There were, of course, a few staid churchmen who threw up their hands in horror at such goings on in a house of men vowed to poverty, chastity, and obedience. But one may think that St. Francis of Assisi, that idealistic, young, and wholly unconventional Italian who is the father and model of the Capuchin friars, would have smiled in his beard at the 'crimes' of his sons. For that work, illegal and criminal though it may have been, was the only work that St. Francis himself recognised as being of value: the work of God. It is true that, in this instance, the 'work of God' seemed very much the work of man. It had none of the trappings of conventional religious endeavours. It did not preach to sinners. It sent out no missionaries. It celebrated no masses, chanted no hours, murmured no prayers. Instead, it saved human lives and salvaged human dignity; and therefore it was blessed and it prospered.

The convent became involved in this work, in the rescue of Jews from the German conquerors of France, almost inadvertently. One day late in 1942 a young woman appeared at the Capuchins' door. She was not the sort of woman whom one normally thinks of as haunting houses of religion. Dressed in the *avant-garde* of fashion, her blond hair in the latest coiffure, poised and composed, she seemed to be what she was: a sophisticated inhabitant of the world of high fashion, sure both of herself and of her place in the cosmos. The aged porter of the convent, unaccustomed to such worldly visions, simply nodded when the woman asked to see Père Marie-Benoît, a professor of theology and of Hebrew in the Capuchin seminary. Then, quickly recovering himself, he added, 'If Madame will be seated in the parlour, I will see if Père Marie-Benoît is at home.'

He led her into a small sitting room, one of those bleak and preternaturally clean cells that one finds in religious houses the world over, and then left her. Once alone, the woman's self-possession seemed to abandon her entirely. Her lips trembling with emotion, she paced the room, adjusting draperies and straightening portraits that had never, since the convent first was built, been askew. It was thus that Father Benoît found her, nervous, ridden with anxiety, unable to remain still for a moment.

'Good evening, madame. You wished to speak with me?'

'Oh, *mon père*—I don't know how to tell you—'

'Please, let us sit. Then we can begin as we should, at the beginning. Now, first, tell me your name.'

The priest's calm voice had its effect. 'I am Fernande Leboucher. It is the name that I use in my profession. My husband's name is Nadelman, Ludwik Nadelman . . .'

'I do not think that I know the name.'

'No, you do not. I have come to see you about Ludwik. He—he is a Jew.'

'I see,' Father Benoît said. And then, gently, although he already knew the answer to his question, he asked, 'And what of your husband?'

'He has disappeared. I am afraid that they have taken him away. You know that they are arresting every Jew that they can find. And Ludwik went out yesterday morning, and I have not seen him or heard from him since. What else can it be?'

The priest and his visitor sat in silence for a moment; then Father Benoît asked quietly, 'And why have you come to me?'

'I have heard that you are a friend to many Jews, that you have helped some who needed help.' Madame Leboucher, for fear of embarrassing the priest, had stated her reason in its most simple form. Indeed, not only she, but all Marseilles, by now had heard that the Capuchin was 'a friend to many Jews.' His special affection for the people of Israel had been awakened as a young seminarian by his study of the Old Testament, and it had grown and been strengthened when, as a young man determined to master the Hebrew language, he had cultivated friendships among the Jewish community of Rome. These friendships had continued when Father Benoît returned to France in 1940 and settled at Marseilles. Through them, and for the sake of them, he had been asked, and had willingly agreed, to provide aid and shelter to various Jewish refugees in that city.

As his reputation had grown, so too had the number of Jews who sought him out to ask his help—help that took the form of food, clothing, money, shelter, and, through his contacts among the Italian authorities in the neighbouring city of Nice, safe-conducts into that part of France under the control of the relatively benign Italian Army. Thanks to these activities, and to his sympathy, his devotion to the Jews, and his practical ingenuity, Father Benoît was known in the city and the surrounding countryside as a man to whom no one appealed for help in vain. It was a reputation of which Madame Leboucher was fully aware before going to the convent, and one on which she counted as her last hope.

The priest, however, was no mere altruist who based his activities and his convictions on a vague humanism. He was a follower of St. Francis of Assisi, that medieval radical who preached, first and always, the revolutionary message of Christ: love. To such men, the concept of 'duty' is not a complex one.

'It is true,' he now explained, 'that I am a friend to the Jews. The Gospels tell us that we are all children of God, and if the Jews are our brothers, how can we not love them? And if we love them, we surely cannot refuse to help them when they need us. You see, it is really quite simple, at least from a theological point of view.

'But from the practical standpoint,' he continued, 'I am afraid that it is more complicated. Occasionally, I have been able to help Jews who were in danger of arrest simply because they were Jews. In such cases, it was not difficult to arrange for them to cross the frontier into Switzerland from the Italian zone, or even into Spain. But your husband—if, as you fear, he has been arrested, I don't know quite how I can be of help. Still —but before talking about that, suppose you tell me what you know about this matter.'

'It is a rather long story, *mon père*, and not always a pleasant one. My husband is an engineer, born in Poland. He came to France when the Germans and the Russians overran his country in 1939. We met shortly after his arrival here, and fell in love. We have not been married long.

'When France fell to the Germans, we came to the Unoccupied Zone, to Marseilles, and rented an apartment here. We had planned to go to America, since we knew that, sooner or later, Hitler would begin persecuting the Jews here, just as he did in Poland. Ludwik has an uncle in New York, and not very long ago we heard from the American consul that he had received an affidavit from the uncle that would make it possible for us to emigrate to the United States. That we have not done so is, I am ashamed to say, because of my foolishness.

'We learned that there were boats available at Saint-Jean-de-Luz, near the Spanish border, to take refugees to England—Jews, especially—and we thought that from England it would be easy to get to the United States. So we went to Saint-Jean-de-Luz with everything that we needed—money, passports, baggage. We were just in time. The ship was to leave the next morning.

'We went to the docks early in the morning, and we found that hundreds of people were already there. They had been waiting since before dawn, to be sure that they would get a place on the boat. The boat itself was anchored in deep water, a good distance from shore, and small fishing boats were supposed to take us from the docks to the ship. At about noon, we all got into these boats—they held only four passengers each—and were taken out to the ship. And that is where the trouble began.

'The only way to board the ship was to climb up a

rope ladder. I am terrified of heights, and the sea was rough; I was certain that, if I tried to climb, I would fall and be drowned. By now, Ludwik and I were the only two passengers left who had not boarded. Those already on the ship were leaning over the railing and trying to encourage me to climb; and the officers were shouting that the ship was already behind schedule, and that if we did not hurry they would have to leave without us.

'The more they shouted, the more frightened I became; and the more frightened I became, the sicker I became. Finally, I was practically paralysed with fear and seasickness, and I knew that I would not be able to move a muscle even to save my life. "I can't do it," I told Ludwik. "You must go alone. I'll follow you later, in some other ship."

'Ludwik refused, but I pleaded and cried and threatened until he agreed that it was the only way. After all, I am a French citizen, a Gentile, and I was in no danger from the Nazis. We embraced, and he turned and began to pull himself up the side of the ship. Halfway up, he stopped; and then he climbed back down. "I can't leave you alone," he said. "If you can't go, then I won't go either." I tried to make him change his mind, but it was too late. Already the rope ladder was being hoisted aboard the ship. And so, we were left there with the fisherman in his boat as the ship moved away toward England. The fisherman merely looked at us, and then shook his head and took us back to shore.'

Madame Leboucher had half expected Father Benoît to react with severity to this confession of her weakness.

Instead, the priest, his face filled with compassion, said only, 'My poor child, how terrible it must have been for you!'

'You can imagine what my feelings were. Because of my silly fears, we had missed the opportunity to get to safety in England, and then to go to America. I expected Ludwik to be furious. Instead, he was kindness itself. He seemed disturbed only because I felt so wretched and so guilty. "No, no," he kept saying, "don't cry. It's perfectly all right. You simply couldn't climb up the ladder, and I simply couldn't leave without you. It's not your fault any more than mine. Besides, it's nothing to worry about. All we have to do is find another way."

'We stayed at Saint-Jean-de-Luz for several days and, to make a long story short, we were offered not one, but two other ways to escape. First, we ran into two Polish officers who had been schoolmates of Ludwik's in Poland. They were about to leave for Marseilles, they told us, where an office had been set up to provide transportation for Polish refugees who wanted to go to England. The second offer came from the French commandant at Saint-Jean-de-Luz. He told us that within a few days a ship would be leaving for Algeria which was controlled by the Free French Forces, and that, if we wished, he would find a place for us on the ship. From Algiers, he pointed out, it would be a simple matter to find a way to Casablanca, and from there to America.

'To me, Algeria seemed the best solution. The important thing was to get Ludwik out of the reach of the Germans; after that, we could worry about getting to the United States. But Ludwik favoured going to Marseilles, where, he argued, the Polish bureau could arrange for us to go directly to America; at Casablanca, he said, we would have to depend on luck in finding a way across the Atlantic. We argued back and forth all day, he with logic and detachment, I with emotion and all the ways that women use in such situations. When I realised that I was losing, I resorted to stratagem and swore that I would not eat again until we were on our way to Algeria. Then, I took to my bed and waited for Ludwik to give in. Several days passed, and still neither one of us would give in. I, because I knew in my heart that, if we returned to Marseilles, it would be the end of Ludwik; Ludwik, out of a mixture of patriotism, loyalty to his Polish friends, and the certainty that the Polish bureau would be able to arrange passage to America for us.

'Finally, I had fasted for so long that I became really ill, and a doctor had to be called in. Still Ludwik did not budge; and so, I gave in. With great misgivings, I agreed that we would go to Marseilles. I had already ruined one opportunity for escape. What if, through my stubbornness, we missed a second chance? I could not take that risk. I packed our suitcases, and we set out.

'In Marseilles again, we went back to our old apartment, which was still vacant. We called it "the pigeon-house," because it was on the top floor and had a small terrace on one side—just like the pigeon-houses that children build. After a day or so, Ludwik began to go out into the city. It was dangerous, but it was the only way to make contact with the Polish organisation. This bureau was a very unusual affair—not a bureau at all, but an illegal underground smuggling operation that specialised in smuggling out Polish refugees who wanted to enlist in the Allied armies. In order to use the organisation, one had first to find it, and then to prove that one was, in fact, a Polish refugee and not a spy for the Germans or an agent of the police. The French government in the Unoccupied Zone has agreed, you recall, to enforce anti-Semitic laws, especially in regard to foreign Jews.'

The priest nodded sadly. 'Yes, I know the laws: unjust, un-Christian, a scandal in a country that considers itself the leader of Western civilisation. But please go on.'

'Well, Ludwik had a good deal of trouble finding the bureau, and then in convincing them that he was a Polish Jew. His Polish friends had disappeared without a trace, and he knew no one else in Marseilles. He became more and more discouraged, and I became more and more worried. I was certain that something dreadful was about to happen. I tried to explain my feeling to Ludwik, but it sounded like nothing more than one of those "premonitions" that women always pretend to have. Then, one morning, Ludwik went out to make what were supposed to be almost the final arrangements for a ship to America. By afternoon, he had not returned. Night came, and still no word from him. I was frantic. I could not sleep, or eat, or think of anything but the certainty that Ludwik had been arrested. I waited all that night for him, and all the next morning. He never came back, and never sent word to me. I waited another day, and still nothing. Then I came here. I don't know what to do. I know hardly anyone in Marseilles, and you were the only one I had heard of who might be able to help.'

Father Benoît sat in silence for a minute, one hand distractedly fingering his Capuchin beard. The story of Ludwik Nadelman and Fernande Leboucher was one that he had heard before, not once but several times, in this very room. The details varied, perhaps, from one telling to the other, and the names of persons and of places shifted, but the basic fact remained the same: a husband, wife, son, or daughter, taken to be sacrificed to the paranoid delusions of an egomaniacal foreign tyrant. Jews, a disconcertingly self-sufficient and tightly knit ethnic group, were being made the scapegoats for every disaster that had befallen Germany in modern times. Hitler called Nazi Germany 'the third *Reich*'— the third empire. He was correct, for it was the third German empire to make a practice of avenging imaginary crimes. From the first empire, the Holy Roman Empire of the Middle Ages, Hitler had inherited the legend of German superiority, the belief that the Teutons were a chosen people, born to rule the world, along with the unofficial anti-Judaism of Roman Catholic tradition. From the second, he had the heritage of Bismarck's belief in 'blood and iron' as the foundation of a strong state, and the tradition of the virulent anti-Semitism of Lutheranism. And now, to that dual inheritance had been added a third factor, that of political expediency: Hitler needed a focal point for the hatreds and resentments of his followers.

A slight movement in the chair opposite him brought Father Benoît back to the problem immediately at hand. 'My dear child, I can understand how you must feel. Tell me, however, if you have checked with the hospitals. Is it possible that your husband might have been involved in an accident and that he has not been arrested at all?'

'I thought of that too, of course, and I called all the hospitals—even the morgue. But I knew what the answer would be. I also thought of asking the police, but I decided that I didn't dare. They might well have his name already, as a foreign-born Jew, and, if I had called, they would have known that he was in Marseilles. It is true that he may have been arrested for some other reason—he might have been involved in a fight, or something like that; but I can't imagine Ludwik taking part in any sort of violence, or doing anything that would cause him to be arrested. It would not be like him.'

'Well, madame, I must confess to you that, at this moment, I don't know quite what to do to help you. It is true, as I've told you, that I've been able to help some refugees, but that was a simple matter—one of finding a place for them to sleep, arranging papers, collecting money for travelling. But to locate someone who may have been arrested—I'm afraid that I have no contacts among the police; and certainly none among the Germans.'

'But surely, *mon père*, there must be a way. Tell me; What happens when a Jew is arrested? Where do they send him?'

'To a place that is called a collection camp,' the priest said. 'You have no doubt heard of them. There are several in the Unoccupied Zone. It is all part of the bargain between the Vichy government and the Germans. In these camps are collected the Jews that the French police, with the not-so-secret help of plain-clothes Gestapo agents, can find. The "internees," as they are called, are held there for a while, sometimes for as long as six or eight weeks. So far as prison camps go, they are not too badly treated; but, of course, the camps are run by the French Army, and not by the Germans. However, I must tell you, madame, that the rest is not pleasant. At regular intervals, the internees are turned over to the Germans, who take them to what they call "distribution centres" in the North of France. From there, the prisoners are sent to Germany as labourers. That is, they are set to work in various factories or on farms, but they live in the famous German concentration camps.'

Madame Leboucher's face reflected the horror implicit in Father Benoît's words, and Father Benoît quickly added, 'You must know these things, madame, and accept them, if we are to help your husband. If he has in fact been arrested, then—but wait; I have just thought of something. If he has been sent to a collection camp, he will be allowed to write and tell you where he is. The French Army and the French police —even Marshal Pétain and his Vichy police—are not Germans. People do not disappear without a trace. If your husband is sent to a collection camp, you may be sure that he will be able to let you know. I think, then, that the only thing for you to do is to wait for a few days more. As soon as you hear from him, come back to see me. Then we'll try to find some way to help him. If you do not hear from him by, let us say, one week

from now, come back in any case. Perhaps between now
and then I will have been able to think of some way to
trace him.'

Madame Leboucher's face mirrored her impatience
at the prospect of simply sitting at home and waiting
for something to happen. 'Isn't there anything useful
that I can do in the meantime?' she asked. 'I hate the
idea of doing nothing while Ludwik——' Here her voice
broke.

Father Benoît, feeling that his visitor had reached the
end of her endurance, felt that he had to reassure her.
'Madame, you said that you came to me because you
had nowhere else to go; that you had heard that I was
in sympathy with my Jewish friends. Now that you are
here, you must trust me. I have seen these things
happen before. If your husband has been arrested, then
you will surely hear from him. If he has not been
arrested, then, for some reason that he considers
sufficient, he is unwilling to contact you for the moment.
It is always possible that he learned, while he was
away from home, that he was in danger of being
arrested, and that he went into hiding. If so, he would
be afraid, naturally, to return home; and he would be
unwilling to send word to you for fear of implicating
you. In that case, he will certainly contact you as soon
as he considers it safe to do so. So, you see, no matter
what may have happened, there is nothing to do but
wait until you hear from him. I am certain, moreover,
that that is what he would want you to do. And you can
be sure that, whatever the case, I will do all in my
power to help you.'

The priest's words were effective. He had spoken in

a gentle voice, but his tone was authoritative. Sensing that the woman felt weak and helpless in the face of an unnamed and faceless terror, he had attempted to give her the strength of a knowledge of alternatives, and the assurance that she did not face those alternatives alone.

Calm again, Madame Leboucher thanked Father Benoît. 'I will do as you say, *mon père*. It will be difficult, but I can see that it is the only way. I will return here as soon as I have heard from Ludwik. And, if I hear nothing, I will return one week from today.'

'Yes, madame. But do not feel that you can do nothing to help Ludwik. I do not know whether you believe in prayer. Even if you do not, make an effort to pray. Ask for help for Ludwik, and for guidance for yourself and for me. You can be sure that, in one way or another, God will answer your prayers. After all, his son was a Jew, too; and he, too, was persecuted during his lifetime. It is not hard to believe that God has a special feeling for the Jewish race.'

'I will try, *mon père*. It is true that I have never prayed much. But then, perhaps I never really needed God before.'

The priest remained standing in the foyer after Madame Leboucher had left. To pray, he reflected, surely that is of the utmost importance. But one must also do something else, something on one's own. It would be wrong to expect God to perform miracles. It was miracle enough that man had been given intelligence and judgement sufficient to solve his own problems. We must work, he determined; we must find some way to help. And, in the meantime, we must pray. 'Work and pray'—the formula for success devised by St. Benedict fifteen hundred years ago. In those simple words lay the solution to every problem. To ask God's help and guidance, that was easy enough; Father Benoît had done that all his life. But to work? How could one 'work' when the whole world seemed to be against what one was working for? Perhaps St. Benedict should have said, 'Pray, pray, pray. And then work.' It seemed that the thing to do, then, was to begin to pray.

For Fernande Leboucher, the days following her visit to Father Benoît were an experience in the un-certainties of human existence. As one day passed, and then another, she oscillated between the extremes of hope and despair: despair that she would ever see her husband again; hope that, with the help of the Capuchin priest, everything would be made right again. At times, as hope faded into doubt, she wept. But at all times she prayed. She prayed, not with rosaries and litanies, but with words from her heart, in a way in which she had not prayed since, as a child about to make her first Communion, life had seemed simple, and heaven and earth had been close together. Alone through the days and the nights, she besieged God: begging, demanding, imploring, threatening; humbly, imperiously, sorrow-fully, proudly.

And then, on the fourth day, the letter came.

The envelope was postmarked, 'Rivesaltes, Pyrénées-Orientales,' and the letter was brief—obviously an 'authorised' communication, subject to censorship. Ludwik informed his wife simply that he had been arrested, and that, as an alien Jew, he was being 'detained' at the Rivesaltes collection camp 'pending disposition of my case.'

Torn between relief and fear, Madame Leboucher hurried to the rue Croix-de-Regnier and showed the letter to Father Benoît.

'It does not tell us much,' he observed. 'But it is enough.'

'Rivesaltes is not a great distance from Marseilles,' Madame Leboucher said. 'Do you think that I will be allowed to visit him?'

'I doubt it. The police are usually very strict about that. Still, in this case—perhaps we are fortunate. As it happens, I know the chaplain at Rivesaltes. I can give you a letter to him. You must go to Rivesaltes and ask to speak with him. Give him the letter—which will merely identify you as a friend of mine—and tell him that I have sent you to him to ask for his help. It is possible that he may be able to obtain permission for you to see your husband. It is a small chance, but it is worth trying.'

'*Mon père*, I want very much to see my husband. But I want more than that to find a way to have him released. I hope that there will be some way—'

'I understand. And, of course, we will do whatever can be done. But first, you must go to Rivesaltes. Once we know what the situation is there, perhaps we can formulate a plan. Come to me as soon as you return to Marseilles, and tell me what you have learned. Then, we will get to work.'

'You are right. That seems the best way.' Now that there was the prospect of action, Madame Leboucher put aside her grief in favour of determination. 'I will go immediately, by the first train. And thank you, *mon père*. I have prayed, as you said, and it would appear that my prayers have been answered, at least in part. I will continue to pray. Perhaps God will suggest a way to free my husband.'

Father Benoît watched her as she walked hurriedly down the busy street. It was hard to believe that this was the distraught, fearful woman who had come to him a few days before. 'I was immensely impressed by her composure and courage in the presence of so dangerous a situation,' he recalled later. 'Yet, after I came to know her better, it seemed entirely natural that she should be so. It is true that, in her heart, she was afraid still; and undoubtedly she was sad. Yet, she was determined, resolved at any price to free her husband. And that resolution seemed a source of limitless strength.'

Madame Leboucher left Marseilles early the next morning. Her destination: Rivesaltes, a small town on the Mediterranean coast some 160 miles west of Marseilles, too unimportant a place to merit regular service by train or autobus. The train took her as far as Perpignan, and then she took a bus, which set her down several miles from the village and the camp. She continued on foot across the countryside, through two miles of disagreeable marshland, and arrived at the camp thoroughly exhausted, her legs caked with mud. Fearfully, she approached the main gate of the camp, holding in her hand the letter from Father Benoît. One of the guards led her inside the enclosure and to the chaplain's office. The priest received her most courteously and, after he had read her letter of introduction, he asked in what way he might be of service.

'Do you think it would be possible for me to see my husband?' she asked.

'It is not generally permitted. Still, you have come a long way, and the commandant is a humane man. I do not think he would have the heart to refuse you. Let us ask him.'

At the office of the commandant, the chaplain spoke for Madame Leboucher. 'This lady, the wife of Ludwik Nadelman, has come from Marseilles to see her husband. He was arrested only recently, and she learned a few days ago that he is here. Naturally, she did not know that no visitors were allowed. I would consider it a personal favour if you were to allow her to see her husband. She is perfectly trustworthy, and she comes highly recommended by a distinguished mutual friend.'

The commander smiled and shrugged, and then wrote out a pass. 'If the clergy cannot refuse to help a beautiful woman, Father, what can you expect of a simple soldier like me?'

For all the French commandant's gallantry, Madame Leboucher was escorted every foot of the way to her husband's barracks by an armed guard with rifle held at the ready. Once there, however, he escorted her to a small room and told her that her husband would be sent for immediately. He left with the admonition, 'You have one half hour, madame.' A few moments later, Ludwik, astonishment on his face, walked into the room.

The couple deluged each other with questions. After Fernande had satisfied her husband's curiosity about how she had been able to get into the camp, she was able to ascertain, first, the details of his arrest, and then to explore the possibility of escape from the camp. As to the first, Ludwik explained that—as he learned too late—the existence of the Polish refugee organisation at Marseilles, and its activities, had been known to the police, and it had been only a matter of time before the Jews who frequented the bureau were picked up. The police had selected the day of his final visit there as a propitious time for a raid. Besides Ludwik himself, a large number of Poles, both Jews and Gentiles, had been caught unawares and arrested. In fact, he explained, several of them were also in the camp.

So far as escape was concerned, it would not be difficult to leave the camp undetected. There was, Ludwik had discovered, a small service road into the camp, which, since it was well concealed, was usually left unguarded. But escape itself would be of little use. As soon as a man was arrested, he was deprived of all ration cards, passports, and other means of identification. And since no one could board a bus or a train, buy food or clothing or medicine, or even safely walk down a street without documents certifying to his name, address, and civil status, it would inevitably only be a matter of hours before any escapee would be caught. The attempt hardly seemed worth the effort—especially since escapees, when caught, were treated with the utmost severity.

Fernande said little as her husband explained these things to her. She merely listened carefully, nodding occasionally; all the while, however, she was thinking. When Ludwik had finished, she asked, 'And if one were somehow to get identification papers, it would be possible then to escape?'

'Yes, I suppose so. The problem is, of course, that they would have to be forged papers. I mean that they would have to have a false name on them. It would do me no good to have papers identifying me as Ludwik Nadelman. I would be back in prison almost immediately. I would have to become someone else—and a Gentile, at that. So you see, it's not a simple matter. I suppose that there is a way to get such papers—through the black market, or through professional forgers, or by bribing someone in the government. But I don't know how one would go about it, and I'm sure that it is extremely dangerous. I would not want you to attempt anything like that. It would only end up with you in prison too.'

'It's not impossible,' Fernande protested. 'There must be a way to go about it that is not so dangerous. I don't know. I'm not sure—but I'm going to find out. I don't want to talk about it, however, until I know for certain whether or not I can do anything. But don't give up hope; it may be just possible—'

At that moment, the guard knocked and entered. 'Your time is up. You'll have to leave now.'

She was allowed a few moments to say good-bye to Ludwik, and then Madame Leboucher was led back to the commandant's office, where she was required to return the pass that she had been given. After thanking the commandant for his kindness, she asked, not without some misgivings, 'Do you think I might come back soon? We've been married only a short time . . .'

'Madame, regulations are very precise on that point. No visitors are allowed at any time. I made an exception in your case today because you had made a long trip,

and because you did not know the rules. However—'
He sighed. 'I suppose that if you came again unexpect-
edly next week I would have to allow you to see your
husband again.' His eyes twinkled. 'I would never hear
the end of it from the chaplain if I didn't.'

The trip back to Marseilles seemed interminable. In
Fernande Leboucher's mind, plans were quickly
formed and just as quickly abandoned. Ineluctably she
was led back to a single conclusion: forged identity
papers, which Father Benoît would have to help her
obtain. But would he be willing? He was a priest, and
to ask him to co-operate in finding forged documents—
surely he would think she was insane to ask such a
thing. Nonetheless, she would have to ask. If he refused,
then she would have to go elsewhere for help, no matter
how dangerous it might be.

With her heart pounding, late that night she presented herself at the Capuchin convent. The startled
porter went to awaken Father Benoît and found him
still awake. He entered the parlour as though midnight
visits from excited women were routine. 'Ah, madame.
You are back. How did it go?'

'Very well, indeed. I mean, as well as it could. Your
friend was able to get me in to see Ludwik, and the
camp commandant has given me permission to go again
next week. I found out how he was arrested.' She gave
the priest the details of her visit, emphasising her conversation with Ludwik about the possibility of escape
and the complications involved in such an attempt. Then
she came boldly to the crux of the matter. 'What he
needs, then, is a new identity, one that the police would

not question—documents of some kind.' She paused.
'I don't know where to find such things. But there must
be a way. Could you possibly suggest anything?'

The Capuchin did not seem alarmed at her question,
or even surprised. Nonetheless, he did not answer immediately, but sat looking out at the darkened street.

'It is difficult for me to ask you, a priest, something
of this kind. Such documents would be illegal, and to
have them would be a crime. Still, if it is the only way
in which I can help Ludwik, then I must do it. I'm
sorry if I've displeased you.'

'My dear friend,' the priest answered, 'it is you who
must forgive me. I did not hesitate because I was unwilling to help you, or because I have any "moral"
objections to the solution that you proposed. The law
under which Ludwik is imprisoned is an immoral one,
and one is not only allowed to ignore such laws but
should actively resist them. There is no doubt in my
mind that this is such a law, and such a time.

'I was merely trying to decide,' he continued, 'what
we can do about a new identity for Ludwik. There are
ways, as you know. All we have to do is decide just
what it is that we want, and then find the appropriate
way of getting it. Now, of course, the best possible
identification would be a passport, but it seems to me
that that would be the most difficult thing to get. They
are complicated documents, and not easy to falsify.

'There is a less difficult way. For one thing, we can
transform Ludwik into a Christian very simply—at
least so far as the police are concerned. All we need do is
get him a certificate of baptism. The Capuchins have
charge of several parishes, and it will be easy to get a

blank form and stamp it with the parish seal. Then we will fill in a new name—a Christian one. That will be enough to establish that he is not a Jew. But that is only half the problem. The certificate of baptism will not be enough to establish a civil identity for him; it will only prove that he is not a Jew. Something else is needed, some sort of official document. Except for the passport —which I think we had better not attempt to get—the best thing would be a ration card. The police accept it as a means of identification readily enough, particularly nowadays when there are so many stateless refugees in the city. I think that that is what we must work on.'

'But where can we go for such a thing? It would have to be a blank,' Madame Leboucher specified, 'so that we can fill in a new name for him. And it would also have to have Ludwik's picture on it.'

'Yes,' the priest said, 'I know. I'm not sure how to go about it. Let me think about it for a day or two, and I will make some inquiries. Come back the day after tomorrow. Perhaps I'll have news by then.'

Father Benoît spent the next two days trying to arrange the proper documentation for Ludwik Nadelman. The baptismal certificate, as he had pointed out to Madame Leboucher, was not a problem. A blank certificate, embossed with the all-important official seal of the church, was his for the asking. By means of it, Ludwik could be presented to the world as a Christian, the son of Christian parents. The ruse would work— so long as the police did not trouble to check the parish registry, for it was not possible to insert an entry into that book substantiating the certificate.

The ration card was something else again. This

small card was difficult to come by because it was precious to every resident of the area of France not occupied by the Germans. Without it, one might be able to identify oneself to the police, but one could buy none of the necessities of life—food, clothing, medicine —and few of the luxuries. Moreover, since it was a generally acceptable means of identification, its distribution was controlled and supervised by the police. In order to obtain one legally, one was required to prove that one was a legal resident of the Unoccupied Zone. There was, however, the black market, where cards supplied by accommodating and impecunious government employees were available, or, failing that, from illegal printing presses. From that source, ration cards were prohibitively expensive.

In the present instance, Father Benoît had no need to resort to the black market. He would have done so if it had been absolutely necessary, but he felt a deep-rooted aversion to men who extorted money in return for the saving of a human life. Now, however, the required document came into his hands with surprising ease. A few telephone calls, a few conversations with men who had been of aid in previous efforts to be helpful to refugee Jews, and he had in his hands one of the precious cards. The place for the bearer's name was blank, but the card carried the official seal—almost certainly forged—of the local prefecture, as well as the necessary tax stamps.

With Madame Leboucher's advice, the certificate of baptism was filled out with a common Christian name, and the ration card completed with the same name and with a photograph of Ludwik. To any observer the documents would have seemed very models of authenticity.

Thus armed, Fernande Leboucher set out again for Rivesaltes, with the certificate and the ration card, because of their incriminating nature, carefully sewn into her skirt.

The commandant of the Rivesaltes camp was as good as his word, and Madame Leboucher was allowed not only to go to her husband's barracks but also to do so without the customary armed guard. As soon as she and Ludwik were alone, she produced the ration card and the certificate. 'Here, look at these! Father Benoît was able to get them through friends. They are already filled out with a fictitious name. Now it will be possible for you to escape. Perhaps you can do it even today. I will meet you in the village, and we'll go together back to Marseilles . . .'

Ludwik had received and inspected the documents with great interest. As his wife hurried on excitedly about her plan, however, he remained quiet and noncommittal. 'A very good job of forging,' he commented. 'This Father Benoît must be a man of talent.'

'What is the trouble, Ludwik? There seems to be something wrong. What is it?'

After some hesitation, Ludwik confided in her. 'I have another plan. What I want you to do is to go back and forth between Marseilles and Rivesaltes a few times in the next two or three weeks. Each time, bring with you as many ration cards as you can get your hands on, and baptismal certificates as well. There is so much to do here, so many people who need help. How can I simply take a card for myself and walk out, leaving the

others to be deported to Germany or to Poland? You
and I, we have our whole lives ahead of us, and there
will be time enough for us. But now we must not think
only of ourselves. We must help these people.'

Madame Leboucher wept and pleaded. And then,
swearing that she would never agree, she agreed. She
recorded later: 'I could refuse nothing to my husband.
He was strong, good, courageous, handsome, and
proud. Moreover, he was right. He would never have
been able to forgive himself if he had deserted his
comrades, while he was able, through me, to provide
the means of escape for at least some of them.'

She carefully explained to her husband, however,
that the ration cards and certificates were not hers to
distribute freely. They would have to come from Father
Benoît, and she did not know how many of them were
available, or even if the priest would agree to supply
them. She promised that she would try her best to do as
Ludwik wished. In return, she exacted a promise from
her husband that he would, if deportation seemed imminent, make use of his own card to escape. 'You will
do no good for yourself or anyone else,' she argued, 'if
you are deported to sit out the war in some concentration
camp or to work in some Polish mine.'

Once the matter had been settled, Ludwik took his
wife on a walk through the camp. They visited the
prisoners' barracks, where she saw men stacked one
above the other in tiers of hammock-like beds, and others
sleeping on the floors with a few blankets thrown over
them. Sometimes, there was a single blanket for two or
even three men. She saw their food being cooked: a pot
of water in which boiled a few beets and peas. And she

saw the faces of the men, lined by fear of the future and
hopelessness for the present, by the prospect of Compound K—the group of small huts, surrounded by
barbed wire, where men were processed for deportation
to Germany as labourers.

And so the day went, until shortly before it was time
for them to part. Then Ludwik took Fernande to his
own barracks. 'I want you to meet some of the men
who need Father Benoît's cards,' he said. 'There are
four of them who must escape very soon. They are
scheduled to be transferred to Compound K in a short
time. I want you to take a good look at each of them. In
Marseilles, you and Father Benoît try to find photographs of all four of them. First of all, ask their
families. I'll give you the addresses before you leave.
If you can't find the families, or if they have no photographs, then you must try to find photographs of men
who resemble them.' She did as he told her, and studied
the men closely. They were pleasant, undistinguished
men, the sort with whom, in other circumstances, one
could have spent happy hours. Now, however, their
presence depressed her, reminded her of where she was,
of where Ludwik was.

When it was time for Fernande to leave, she tried,
for her husband's sake, to appear gay, but in her heart
she was inexpressibly sad. 'Be strong,' Ludwik whispered. 'Do not lose your courage. You must go, and I
must remain here. Together, we must do what we can
to save these men.'

She left with her mind filled by the vision of those
rows of cold, unpainted wooden barracks. On the train
ride back to Marseilles, she could not put out of her

mind the thought of Ludwik in that bleak, desolate place, and a feeling of hopelessness flooded her. Yet, at the same time, she could not resist a strange sense of pride—pride in her husband's strength, courage; in his determination to help his fellow prisoners rather than to save himself. And from the despair and the pride there emerged a firm resolution. She would never give up until she and Ludwik were once again united and free.

Hours later, she arrived in Marseilles. Though exhausted, she went immediately to the Capuchin convent to report to Father Benoît. There she explained to the priest her husband's plan of escape for his fellow prisoners, while he sat listening attentively, interrupting occasionally only to ask a question or to make a comment. When she had finished, he unhesitatingly expressed his enthusiasm for the plan, and his eagerness to co-operate in it.

'It will require a good deal of thought to devise a safe, steady supply of the ration cards,' he said. 'But I think that, with the help of friends, we can do it. But we cannot stop there. We must also do something for the men after they have escaped. It will not be enough for them to get out of the camp. They must have a place in which to stay until we can get them safely out of the country, and they must have food, and shelter, and clothing, and money.'

'I had not thought of those things,' Fernande admitted. 'Can they be arranged?'

'I think so. There are many homes in Marseilles that are willing to take in refugee Jews. I know people who —but let me get to work on it. The four ration cards should be obtainable somehow, and I can get the baptismal certificates at any time. I will also find temporary hiding places for the four men, and later on we can think about a way to get them into Spain or Italy. I am sure that my old contacts will be useful in that respect.'

The two sat into the small hours of the morning, discussing, planning. When Madame Leboucher at length returned home and fell exhausted onto her bed.

'Now,' she thought, 'I shall do something.' And then she drifted into sleep. It never occurred to her that she had set the Capuchin priest on an adventure that was to fill his life for years to come; that the humble monk was to live henceforth in jeopardy, a criminal who would fight, plot, conspire, cajole, plead, threaten, and lie for the sake of his crime: the saving of thousands of Jews from the certain death of Nazi imprisonment, torture, and death.

2

The Background

THERE was little in the background of Père Marie-Benoît to indicate that he was born to work heroic deeds, but there was a great deal to suggest the formation of a character within which courage and devotion would supply the fabric of heroism. His roots, like those of most of the French clergy, were in the sturdy, hard-working bourgeoisie of provincial France. 'I am,' he wrote, 'the product, so to speak, of two flour mills. My father was the local miller at Pommeraie, Maine-et-Loire, and my mother's family operated the flour mill in the nearby town of Tremblay, Maine-et-Loire. One might say that I had flour in my blood.'

The mill at Pommeraie had been, for as long as anyone in the neighbourhood could remember, the property of the Peteul family, until Pierre Peteul—Marie-Benoît's father—withdrew from the business in 1900. The Peteuls, indeed, had lived in the northeast corner of Anjou (the modern department of Maine-et-Loire) in western France for centuries, where they were widely known as a solid, hard-working clan, devoted to their religion and to their country. One ancestor of Marie-Benoît, Angélique Peteul, is remembered as a martyr to her religious and political loyalties during the French Revolution. It is recorded that she was executed because she had 'opposed the death of Capet [i.e., Louis XVI], and, being a fanatic and a hypocrite, she preferred refractory priests [those who refused to take an oath of allegiance to the Revolution at the expense of their loyalty to Rome] to the others.'

This devotion to Roman Catholicism seems to have characterised the Peteul family from that day forward. An uncle of Marie-Benoît, who was also named Marie-Benoît, was the eldest of thirteen children, four of whom entered the religious life. The uncle himself became a Trappist monk at the Abbey of Bellefontaine, where he is still spoken of as a model of monastic virtue. 'He has but one passion,' it was said, 'and that is for the Gregorian chant. If he has others, then he is master of them, for he is the very exemplar of virtue.' The monk was sent to Canada, where he was one of the founders of the monastery of Oka, and where he died, at the age of thirty-two, as the result of a pneumonia contracted while carrying the last sacraments to a dying woman. 'His death was as gentle and holy as his life,' it was written. 'If it is as difficult as is believed to live as a Trappist, it is nonetheless easy to die as one, and he died while reciting a hymn from the Office of the Virgin Mary.'

The memory of this saintly uncle and of his martyred forebear was not lost on young Pierre Peteul, as Père Marie-Benoît was known before his entry into religious life. When he was five years old, his family moved to the city of Angers; it was there, a few years later, that he heard a sermon on that most sympathetic and heroic of saints, Francis of Assisi, the founder of the Franciscan Order. From that moment, at the age of twelve, Pierre Peteul knew what he was to make of his life. Before very long, he was studying for the priesthood in the Capuchin Order, a reformed branch of the Franciscans that dates from the sixteenth century.

At the time that Pierre was in the seminary, the Government of France was not kindly disposed either to religion or to religious orders in particular. It was a time of vehement anti-clericalism, a phenomenon that manifested itself at all levels, political as well as social and intellectual. Many priests and religious found it necessary to go into hiding, or to leave the country; and religious schools and seminaries, particularly, were frowned upon and discriminated against. In 1907, therefore, Pierre Peteul left France for Belgium, where, at the town of Spy, he enrolled in a minor seminary. He remained there for six years while finishing his classical studies, and then, in 1913, he went to Holland and was admitted to the Capuchin novitiate at Breust-Eijsden. Like every other novice, Pierre spent the entire year in learning the basic discipline of the religious life: prayer. The next year, he took his first, or temporary, vows of poverty, chastity, and obedience. At the same time, the newly made monk, according to Church custom, was given a new name, one reflecting his 'birth to a new life.' It happened that an article on Pierre's uncle, the Trappist monk Marie-Benoît, had recently appeared in a Catholic magazine, and Pierre's superiors were inspired by it to christen the nephew in honour of the uncle. 'In memory of your saintly uncle, you shall hereafter be known as Marie-Benoît,' he was told. And it was as Marie-Benoît that Pierre Peteul was to make his mark on his times.

In September of the same year, Marie-Benoît began his studies in philosophy, a preparation for theology that Church law requires be pursued for two years. In January 1915, however, academic occupations were interrupted for a general mobilisation. World War I had broken out. When Germany moved to occupy Belgium, the young novice fled first to England, and then, shortly afterward, back to France. Within a few days he had enlisted in the Army and, after a brief period of training, he was assigned to the 44th Infantry Regiment, in which he served as a medical orderly, a stretcher-bearer, and a rifleman on various fronts: the Somme, Verdun, and Alsace. In the course of these campaigns, the monk-turned-soldier received five citations for bravery under fire. The laws of chance, however, pursue even the brave, and in September 1917 Marie-Benoît was wounded during the Battle of Verdun. He was allowed two months to recuperate and, by the end of the year, he was again in the trenches of northern France.

By the middle of 1918, France's officer corps had been decimated by four years of bitter war, and there was issued a general call for volunteers to take their places. Marie-Benoît submitted his name, and he was accepted and assigned to a machine-gun training school near Poitiers. By the time the armistice was signed, on November 11, 1918, he had finished the courses there and been transferred to Morocco, where he was assigned to the 15th Algerian Rifle Regiment. In the following year, Marie-Benoît's period of enlistment expired, and he was honourably discharged from the service as a lieutenant.

After a brief visit to France, Marie-Benoît returned to Holland to resume his theological studies. Shortly afterwards, being an outstanding student, he was sent to Rome to complete his courses, and he was ordained there in 1925. In the same year, he was granted the degree of Doctor of Sacred Theology. From that time until 1939, he remained in Rome as Professor of Theology at the Collège International de St. Laurent.

When war broke out, in 1939, with France and England on one side and Germany on the other, Marie-Benoît returned to France, where, like most Frenchmen of his age, he was recalled to active duty in the Army. He was assigned as Italian interpreter to the headquarters of General Gillotte, commander of the Southeast Army Group. The mission of this group was to attack the German rear by crossing into Austria by way of Italy—for Italy at that time was thought to be well disposed to the Allies. After circumstances had made it clear that Mussolini's sympathies lay with Hitler rather than with France and England, all hope of his cooperation in General Gillotte's mission was abandoned, and the general was then transferred to the North of France. Marie-Benoît, in the helter-skelter manner in which such things are handled in all armies, was transferred along with him, still as an Italian interpreter. It was soon discovered, however, that there was little use for an Italian interpreter in the North of France, and

Marie-Benoît was thereupon reassigned to a head-quarters near the Franco-Italian frontier.

In wartime, confusion becomes chaos, and the simple inefficiencies of peacetime are transformed into imbecilic incompetence. Marie-Benoît learned this lesson quickly enough, for no sooner was he back in the South of France than he was told that his recall into the service had been a mistake in the first place. As a resident of Italy, he was informed, he should have remained in that country and reported for duty to the nearest French military attaché. He was then ordered to return to Italy and to present himself at the office of the military attaché at the French embassy in Rome. He did so in 1940.

That fateful year is not one that any Frenchman can easily forget. The first part of 1940 was during the time of the 'phony war,' as it was called by the Allies, or the *sitzkrieg* ('sit-down war') as the Germans called it—a period in which the Allies and the Germans held still and each waited for the other to move. Poland had fallen, and the Germans had gained control of Denmark and Norway. Hitler, now that he had taken what he wanted—i.e., Poland—seemed disinclined to continue the war. 'I have no war aims against Britain and France,' he declared. 'They can still have peace if they want it—but they will have to hurry.' Neither Britain nor France hurried, for the peace that Hitler offered was predicated on their acceptance of what Hitler regarded as 'the legitimate fruits of victory.'

In May of 1940, therefore, the *sitzkrieg* was suddenly replaced by the *blitzkrieg*, and the war began in earnest. German armies overran Holland and Belgium

and then swung toward France. That country, hope-
lessly divided, her armies ill equipped, many of her
eighty divisions of little value, succumbed almost immediately to the numerically inferior, but tactically
superior, forces of Nazi Germany. On June 16, the
French government, under Marshal Pétain, surrendered
formally to Germany.

Only six days before, Mussolini's Italy, sensing the
direction of the wind, had declared war on France.
'Mussolini,' as one historian puts it, 'thrust his small
dagger into France's back.' To be sure, the Italian
intervention had little effect upon the German position
in France, or upon the condition of France herself. It
did affect, however, the large French community of
residents in Italy, who were declared to be 'alien belligerents' and ordered to leave Italy immediately.

The France to which these men and women returned
was a strange one. Paris, of course, was occupied by the
Germans, as was all of the northern part of the country
and all of the Atlantic coast. Hitler had left to the puppet
French government of Marshal Pétain, established at
Vichy, an unoccupied zone in the south and southeast,
which it was to be free, at least superficially, to govern.
The purpose of this division of France into 'occupied'
and 'unoccupied' zones was to render difficult the
formation of a French government-in-exile, and to
prevent the removal of French civilian authority to one
of the French colonies in North Africa. Moreover, Hitler
was not unaware that the rulers of the Unoccupied
Zone—Pétain, General Weygand, and Pierre Laval—
were no friends of democracy, and that they would be in
a better position to help him establish his New Order

in Europe as masters of a 'sovereign' state than as openly subservient figureheads in a wholly occupied France.

Hitler was not about to share the fruits of victory with Mussolini, the latecomer. The Italian dictator demanded as his share the great ports of Toulon and Marseilles on the Mediterranean coast of France, as well as a sizable strip of the Riviera. What he got was the few hundred square miles of French territory that his troops had managed to occupy while the French were otherwise engaged in the north. As a token of goodwill, he was also granted control of a fifty-mile-wide 'demilitarised zone' between Italy and France, an area containing the city of Nice.

Père Marie-Benoît, who was among the French 'alien belligerents' deported from Italy, was at first undecided as to a course of action. He could not return to the Capuchin headquarters in Paris, for that city was under the thumb of the Nazis. He could not rejoin the French Army, for the latter by now had been all but dispersed. He therefore elected to go to Marseilles, in the Unoccupied Zone of France and near to the Italian sector.

It was a fortuitous choice. Marseilles was, and was to become even more, a gathering place for the refugees of Europe. Jews from Poland, particularly, and from all of Eastern Europe flocked to the great seaport in hopes of being able to make their way from there to England or to America or, failing that, to be able to find a means of crossing over into near-by Switzerland or Spain. Moreover, the proximity of the Italian zone of France, where an official anti-Semitism was reputed to be neutralised by an unwillingness to implement Mussolini's discriminatory laws, offered a further inducement to homeless Jews in search of an easily accessible haven. The city therefore thronged with Jews, many of them with their families, most of them friendless and penniless, and almost all of them desperate for a means of escape. It was not long before Père Benoît came into contact with these victims of Hitler's paranoia, and, very shortly, he was actively engaged in refugee-relief work among them—finding food and shelter for them, soliciting funds on their behalf, and smoothing the way over administrative hurdles into the near-by neutral countries.

As he worked, he learned; and his sympathy for his Jewish friends had grown apace with his horror of the Nazi doctrine of racial superiority. The unhappy fact of anti-Semitism in Europe was not new to him, of course. He had seen it promulgated on a national scale in Germany, and his studies had acquainted him with similar phenomena throughout history. The ancient Romans had had their pogroms; and the Fathers of the Church—St. John Chrysostom, for example, and St. Cyprian—had denounced the 'perfidious Jews' in terms that would remain unequalled in vehemence until Luther took up the cudgel more than a thousand years later. Thanks to such reasoning, a strong dose of anti-Semitism was injected into the bloodstream of the Church. A curious admixture of emotional aversion and theological condemnation, it made hatred of the Jews seem an unofficial tenet of Christian belief. The medieval Crusaders, for example, made a regular practice of massacring European Jews by the thousands —'the infidels among us,' they called them—before setting off to fight the Saracens in the Holy Land. Such pogroms were not uncommon even at other times during the Middle Ages in England, Germany, and Spain.

It is one of the ironies of history that, while Christians all over Europe were killing Jews by the tens of thousands, 'in the name of Christ the King,' the most constant protector of the Jews was the Pope, the successor of the Jewish fisherman named Peter. A bull of Pope Calixtus II, *Sicut Judaeis*, issued in 1120, which strongly condemned attacks upon Jews and their baptism under threat of violence, was confirmed and re-promulgated twenty-three times before the end of the fifteenth century.

Despite such papal efforts, freedom for the Jews first appeared in lands that had, during the Reformation, broken away from Rome—in Holland and in England, particularly. The Catholic states of France and Austria, and the Protestant one of Prussia followed suit by the end of the eighteenth century. Jews resident in those countries were accepted as full and equal citizens, on a par with their Gentile compatriots.

In Italy, however, the new spirit did not arrive until it was forcibly introduced by Napoleon Bonaparte. During the course of his victorious march across the peninsula, the gates of Venice's ghetto were removed and destroyed. At Rome, Bonaparte liberated the Jews and caused two of them to be elected to the governing council of the city. Yet, after Napoleon's fall in 1815, the Jews of the Papal States soon found themselves once more the victims of oppression. The establishment of Mazzini's Roman Republic in 1849, during which Pope Pius IX was forced to flee the city, left the pontiff frightened and sour. Henceforth, his liberal principles were replaced by the unshakable conviction that only an inflexible exercise of authority could prevent the erosion of religious dogma by the pernicious modern beliefs of liberty, equality, and fraternity. Upon his return to Rome, the Jews were once more clapped into the ghetto. It was not until 1870 that the Roman ghetto was finally abolished, by order of the conqueror of the city, Victor Emmanuel II, and the Jews of the former Papal States were able to exercise their rights as citizens of Italy.

The papacy, however, though shorn of its political power and its temporal possessions, still retained its spiritual authority; and it was not long before that authority began to be used to disseminate hatred for the Jews. During the reign of Leo XIII (1878–1903), a campaign of outspoken anti-Semitism was openly waged in the Catholic journals of Italy, official as well as unofficial. The most vehement of these was *Civiltà Cattolica*, the official organ of the Society of Jesus (the Jesuits), which published numerous articles on the subject. Readers were informed that the Jews had been the instigators of the French Revolution, and that the principle of 'liberty, equality, fraternity' was nothing more than an illusion conjured up in order to guarantee the civil rights of Europe's Jews. Moreover, the Jews of all the liberal states were participants in a campaign to 'dominate the key positions in most national economies' so as to perpetuate their 'virulent campaigns against Christianity.' The long-range intention of the Jews was to 'take control of the whole world.'

No human act is without consequence in the chain of

historical causality. Hitler's anti-Semitism, rooted though it may have been in centuries of tradition and legend, could not have flourished as it did if it had existed in a vacuum. Unfortunately, there was no vacuum; far from it. The flames of intolerance, which had been kindled by ecclesiastical attitudes and fed by the ambitions of self-serving politicians such as Hitler's admired Karl Lueger, now threatened to spread throughout Europe. The Russian Revolution of 1917 added new fuel to the fire. Although the Jews of Russia suffered enormously in the Bolshevik take-over of that country, it was stated throughout Europe that the revolution was part and parcel of an 'international Jewish conspiracy.' The simple-minded accepted as evidence the fact that Karl Marx, the prophet of atheistic communism, had been born a Jew. That Marx had become a Christian early in childhood, and that he himself was a bitter anti-Semite, were ignored, and the term 'Jewish Bolshevism' came into common usage in Europe and America. The irreconcilable *Civiltà Cattolica* immediately took up the cry, as did Catholic publications in Austria, Italy, and Germany. Even the normally staid *Osservatore Romano* headlined an editorial of November 27, 1929, 'The Jewish Threat to the World.'

In this climate it was not hard for Hitler—busy at work in the 1920s with the organisation of his National Socialist Party in Germany—to find a slogan behind which to rally the defeated and despondent German people. The Jews and the Marxists, he preached, had been the 'invisible foes' of Germany during the World War; it was to the tactics of the Jewish financiers and industrialists of Germany that the German Empire owed its defeat by the Allies. 'In the years 1916 and 1917,' he wrote, 'the whole of production was under the control of Jewish finance. . . . The Jew robbed the nation and pressed it beneath his domination. I saw with horror the approach of a catastrophe.' And thus Hitler whispered into the ears of the defeated German nation a beguiling myth: that of the 'stab in the back.' Germany had not been defeated on the field by the Allies in 1918; she had been stabbed in the back by traitors at home—meaning, of course, the Jews. The Jews, therefore, must be 'dealt with.'

To many Europeans, Hitler's proposed programme of Jewish repression seemed nothing more than an exercise in political rhetoric. They were to learn otherwise. No sooner had Hitler been appointed to the chancellorship of the Reich than his programme was put into effect. As he had so often declared, the Jews were not Germans and they had no right to be treated as Germans. He promulgated laws banning them from public service, from the universities, and from the professions. On April 1, 1933, he declared a national boycott of Jewish shops. In the meanwhile, of course, thousands of Jews were robbed, beaten, and murdered in the streets by Nazi storm troopers while the police looked on indifferently. Hitler's wish, as Hermann Goering realistically observed, was now Germany's only law.

This was merely a beginning. Hitler's long-range plan was to make Germany *Judenrein*—'free of Jews.' On the night of November 9, 1937, the most savage pogrom that had occurred in Germany since the

Crusades took place. Synagogues, and Jewish homes, offices, and shops were burned to the ground. Some twenty thousand Jews were arrested and herded into concentration camps. Some seventy-five hundred shops were looted. Of the perpetrators of these crimes, only those who had raped Jewish women were punished, for they had violated the law forbidding sexual intercourse between Gentiles and Jews. A few days after the pogrom, a decree was announced eliminating Jews from the German economy and robbing them of what was left of their property.

The ultimate purpose of such persecution, the notorious 'final solution' of Hitler, was nothing less than the extermination of Europe's Jews. The Jews were the *Untermenschen*—the subhumans—of Europe; as such, they had no right to live.

By 1940, when Père Marie-Benoît established himself at Marseilles, the Republic of France, the home of Europe's largest Jewish population, was in danger of falling victim to Hitler's determination to rid the continent of the 'scoundrels.' Soon after France's fall, anti-Semitic laws were promulgated. Jews were deprived of the rights of citizenship; they were required to register as Jews; all Jewish businesses and shops were to be clearly marked as such; a strict curfew was enforced; and all Jews were required to wear a distinguishing badge. Numerous 'collection camps' were constructed, to be used in the rounding up and deportation of Jews to Germany as slave labour and, later, as material for Hitler's death chambers at Buchenwald, Dachau, etc. To assure the success of this programme, Adolf Eichmann himself, the head of the Gestapo's 'Jewish

Office'—and therefore the man immediately responsible for the implementation of Hitler's 'policy of extermination'—journeyed to Paris to supervise the preparations.

France, however, was not Germany; or, more accurately, Frenchmen were not Germans. France had had its share of anti-Semitism in the past, in the famous Dreyfus case of the early 1900s, for example; but French Jews had not inhabited ghettos for centuries, and now, in most instances, they were virtually indistinguishable —except for religious beliefs—from the rest of the population. They regarded themselves, and they were regarded by French Christians, simply as Frenchmen of the Jewish faith. Political hatred was easy to stir up in France, and occasionally religious bias reared its head. But the French generally—a race whose colonists had casually and unselfconsciously intermarried with 'natives' of all colours the world over—were little susceptible to the virus of racism in any form. It was France that had been the first country of Europe to enfranchise its Jews and to admit them to public office. Jewish prime ministers had ruled France, Jewish chief justices had adjudicated her internal disputes, and Jewish generals had commanded her armies.

This liberal tradition was sufficiently strong to give pause to Marshal Pétain, head of France's German-controlled Vichy government, when Hitler required that anti-Semitic laws be adopted in the Unoccupied Zone of France. Before acting, he queried his ambassador at the Vatican, Léon Bérard, concerning the papal attitude toward German treatment of the Jews. M. Bérard replied in a letter that remains one of the curiosities of the Second World War for its peculiar admixture of theological inflexibility with humane generosity:

> We know from history that the Catholic Church has often protected Jews from violence and injustice by their persecutors, while at the same time relegating them to the ghettos. . . . St. Thomas Aquinas, in his *Summa Theologica,* sums up the matter as follows: The Jews must be allowed the exercise of their religion, and they must be protected from religious coercion. . . . Still, it would be unreasonable for a Christian state to allow Jews to participate in the government, since this would subject Catholics to Jewish authority. It therefore follows that it is legitimate to forbid them acess to public office. . . . The Vatican, however, has expressed the wish that the precepts of justice and charity be observed in the application of the law.

In the Unoccupied Zone, so long as it remained unoccupied, the spirit of this advice was observed. The *Status des Juifs,* as the anti-Jewish laws were called, were indeed promulgated, but they were leniently enforced, in accordance with 'the precepts of justice and charity.' Even French collaborators with the Germans —and there were more than a few of them—shrank in horror from Eichmann's talk of extermination. French Jews, they pointed out, were, after all, Frenchmen, and, as such, they could not be sacrificed to the unreasonable demands of a foreign government. Eichmann, however, had to be pacified, and an accommodation was reached. The Germans were willing to accept a 'partial solution' to the Jewish problem in

France, whereby only non-French Jews would be deported from the country. Some twenty thousand stateless Jews—most of whom had come to France from Germany and Eastern Europe to escape from the Germans—were rounded up in the collection camps and prepared for shipment to Germany. Three times, transports were scheduled; and three times they had to be cancelled because of mysterious 'mechanical failures' that were discovered only at the last minute. Eichmann, enraged at the desultory manner in which the French police were pursuing the Jews, and at the high rate of escape from the collection camps, threatened to drop France as an area from which Jews were to be evacuated and to treat the Jews there as they had been treated in Poland—that is, herded together and shot.

Under the impetus provided by this threat, which no one doubted for a moment Eichmann to be perfectly capable of carrying out, the means of transportation were finally found and the first detachment of Jews was deported to the east amidst a general feeling of frustrated anger among the French. The clergy of the country, unlike that of Germany, was not afraid to speak its mind, and on that occasion the parish churches in many towns and cities resounded with the indignation of the priests and bishops. Particularly outspoken was Msgr. Saliège, Archbishop of Toulouse, who drew up a pastoral letter that he ordered to be read from every pulpit of his archdiocese:

There exists a human system of morals which both imposes certain duties and recognises certain rights. These rights and these duties come equally from

God. They may be ignored, but they can never be destroyed. . . . Children, mothers, and fathers have been treated like animals. That the members of a family can be separated from one another and shipped like cattle to unknown destinations is one of the tragic spectacles of our day. . . . In our own archdiocese, horrible scenes are taking place in the collection camps of Noe and Recebedou. Jews are men. Jews are women. They form part of the family of mankind. They are our brothers, a fact that Christians must not forget. France, our beloved France, which nourishes in the consciences of her children a tradition of respect for the individual; France, the generous and the chivalrous—she is not responsible for these horrors. . . .

The Prefect of Toulouse, of course, soon heard of this public denunciation, and he lost no time in demanding that the archbishop publish a retraction. Saliège replied indignantly, 'It is my duty to instruct my people in good morals; and when it becomes necessary, I shall do so even for officials of the government.' The prefect then attempted to forbid the reading of the letter, but his order was universally ignored, and the letter—which had now become known as 'the Saliège bomb'—was not only read from the pulpit, but duplicated and widely distributed throughout France. Copies were even found in German prison camps. It was read on the B.B.C. stations and on Vatican Radio and reprinted in the *Osservatore Romano*. The Vichy government was outraged, and Pierre Laval requested the papal nuncio to call the matter to the attention of the

Pope, Pius XII, and warned him that the government was determined 'not to allow interference of this sort in the internal affairs of France.'

The climax of the affair of the 'Saliège bomb,' however, occurred a few days later. Two German plainclothes policemen knocked at the door of the archbishop's residence in Toulouse and asked to speak with him. When admitted to his office, they brusquely ordered him to come with them to Gestapo headquarters. Quietly the archbishop took his hat and overcoat, and then summoned his housekeeper, an aged religious named Sister Henriette, who was famous in Toulouse for her devotion to the archbishop and for the sharpness of her tongue.

'Sister,' the archbishop said, 'I am going away with these gentlemen. I do not know when I shall return. Please see that things remain as they are during my absence.'

Sister Henriette, who had been known to spare not even the archbishop himself when her temper was aroused, was not about to give in to mere Germans. 'Are you out of your minds?' she shrieked at the startled men. 'Do you know that he is 75 years old? Can't you see that he cannot even walk without a stick? I tell you, if you take him out of this house, you will kill him, and you'll be the ones responsible for his death!'

The Germans may have been old parochial-school boys in whom the fear of 'Sister's wrath' had never entirely died. Or they may simply have been astute enough to realise that the death of an archbishop in a German prison would have an adverse effect upon public opinion and upon the Reich's ever-worsening relations with the Vatican. In any case, after a hurried consultation, they left, saying, 'We will come back to-morrow.' But they never returned.

As Eichmann's henchmen rounded up more stateless Jews—over twelve thousand in Paris alone—other prelates followed the example set by Saliège. The bishops of Albi, Montauban, Marseilles and Nice protested that anti-Semitic measures were 'a violation of human dignity and of the sacred rights of the in-dividual and the family,' and proclaimed that 'all men are brothers, created by one God.' A joint proclamation, initiated by Cardinal Suhard of Paris and subscribed to by all the bishops of Occupied France for submittal to Marshal Pétain, stated:

> Profoundly shocked by the mass arrests and the in-human treatment meted out to Jews, we cannot silence the outcry of our consciences. In the name of humanity and in that of Christian principles, we must protest in favour of the inalienable rights of man. . . .

This protest, however, was without issue, and the arrests continued throughout France. On one occasion, Eichmann's henchmen arrested six Jewish families at Lyons, but the French police refused to separate those to be deported from their children, and they gave the deportees one hour to decide whether or not they wished to take their children with them. The news immediately reached Cardinal Gerlier, the archbishop, who offered to take the Jewish children into his house and under his protection. The Jewish parents agreed, and the cardinal promised to provide the children with food and clothing, and to supervise their education. He also voluntarily promised, in writing, that no attempt would be made to convert the nine children to Catholicism. Four days later, the Prefect of Lyons, at Eichmann's orders, presented himself at the cardinal's office and demanded that the children be turned over to him. Gerlier answered frostily, 'If I were to comply with your demand, then I should no longer be worthy to be Archbishop of Lyons. Good day, sir.'

Gerlier moreover defied both French and German authorities by publicly expressing sympathy to the Chief Rabbi of France when, in October 1941, the Germans attempted to burn the synagogues of Paris. 'Catholics,' he wrote, 'are profoundly affected by the tragedy that has fallen upon the people of Israel.' Subsequently, he called upon all French Catholics to refuse to surrender to the Germans the hidden children of deported Jews.

Apparently, it was not necessary for him to exhort them to offer such shelter. A Jewish member of the French underground, Léon Poliakov, recorded: 'Priests, members of religious orders, and laymen were rivals in giving shelter to Jews, thereby saving honour of French Catholics. And, in saving their honour, they also saved the lives of tens of thousands of Jews.'

The Nazis, of course, were aware of this alliance between Christians and Jews. One Nazi journal, after demanding the head of Gerlier as 'a raving Talmudist, traitor to his faith, to his country, and to his race,' announced: 'We are facing a proper declaration of war by several of the princes of the Church. We have no illusions. The alliance between the ecclesiastical up-

starts and the Jews is now complete.' One Nazi
journalist discovered that 'every Catholic family shelters
a Jew. Even the French authorities provide the Jews
with forged papers and passports, and priests help
them across the Swiss frontier.' As a direct result of such
defiance by the French clergy, Pierre Laval ordered
that all Catholic priests who hid Jewish children in
their rectories were to be arrested. Within two months,
about one hundred and twenty-five such men were imprisoned at Metz, and then deported eastward 'to
unknown destinations.' Most of them were never heard
from again.

As mass deportations reached a climax, in August
1942, the Papal Nuncio, Archbishop Valerio Valeri,
appealed to the government to 'temper the severity of
the measures taken against the Jews.' When no answer
was received, he protested in stronger terms to Marshal
Pétain: 'The Holy Father himself asks that you put an
end to these inhuman arrests of defenceless people.'
When Pétain replied that it was his hope that the Pope
would understand and approve of his position, Valeri
retorted, 'Monsieur, the Holy Father can neither understand it nor approve of it.' Eventually, the protest was
rejected by the government, with the comment that the
government 'could not be influenced by the Holy See.'

German cruelty and the subservience of the French
government served only to provoke the priests of
France to greater effort on behalf of the Jews. A priest
of the Society of Our Lady of Zion saved, almost single-
handed—by shipping them across neutral borders—
some six hundred and fifty Jews. Another priest, R. P.
Fleury, performed the same service for several hundred

Jewish children of Poitiers. A nun, Sister Alice Fer-
rière, concealed and cared for a group of fifteen Jewish
children from 1941 to 1944. Such acts of courageous
charity were common among the clergy and laity of
France, both Protestant and Catholic. Children and
adults were hidden by the thousands all over France.
Jews who had never seen the interior of a Catholic
church suddenly found themselves living in the ancient
monasteries and bleak convents of France, clothed in
the flowing habits of the ancient orders, while their
children, decorated by Christian names and 'rehabili-
tated' by means of forged baptismal certificates,
mingled unnoticed with French children in schools,
institutions, and homes.

It was a vast operation, and a disorganised one.
Rescuers worked alone, or in groups of two or three, or,
occasionally, within a network of other rescue workers.
Not infrequently, both clergy and laymen were caught
in the act, and they were deported, or disappeared into
prisons. Many of them died of neglect, or were killed;
but many survived to tell the tale of their adventures.
And many who were under the eye of the Gestapo
escaped to continue their work elsewhere.

Among the latter was Père Marie-Benoît.

3

The Rescue

I T required a few days' work on the part of Father
Benoît and Fernande Leboucher to assemble the
documents needed for the prisoners at Rivesaltes. First
in the order of priority, and by far the most difficult,
were the ration cards. To obtain one such was a major
undertaking, involving grave risks. Obtaining four
ration cards was a project of such dimensions and complications that there seemed to be only one possible
source: the French Resistance. These patriots, bound
together in a well-organised and highly efficient
system, had cells in every major French city as well as
in many towns and villages, and their contacts were
everywhere. Their mission was, simply, 'resistance'—
to the Germans and to the work of the Germans; and
their *modus operandi* was one of sabotage on every level,
administrative as well as military and economic. For
that purpose, Resistance agents had infiltrated the
offices of the Vichy government and the police, and, with
the help of this many-tentacled organisation, almost
anything that was not completely beyond the bounds of
possibility could be accomplished.

Father Benoît had had some contact with the
Resistance in his work with the Jews prior to this time,
and he had maintained his relationships among its
members. Now, he felt, it was time to take advantage of
those contacts.

The method to be followed in working with the
Resistance was itself rather complicated. No one knew
everyone in the Resistance, for such knowledge—even
if it had covered only the agents, say, in a city such as
Marseilles—would have been extremely dangerous.
The Gestapo were very competent in extracting information from even the most unwilling lips. Father Benoît
therefore had to get in touch with his 'contact'—a man
who might be anything from a dock worker to an
archbishop. The contact, in turn, had other contacts,
to whom he passed on the request for ration cards.
They, in turn, transmitted the information, in an ever-
widening circle, until it reached a Resistance agent—
in this case, a government employee—who was in a
position either to steal or, preferably, to obtain legally,
the four cards. The cards were then passed from hand
to hand, down the line, until they reached Father Benoît.
At no time did the recipients know the ultimate source
of the cards; and thus, the source was protected from
disclosure of his identity if any of the recipients were
arrested and questioned.

In the meantime, Fernande Leboucher was busy with
the photographs. Two of the families were located, and
photographs of the men were obtained. For the other
two, however, it was necessary to depend on the ac-
curacy of Fernande's memory, and photographs were
found of people who resembled, in a general way, the

men for whom the ration cards were destined. This seemed a fairly safe procedure, Fernande felt, since official identity photographs rarely bear much resemblance to the subject.

Once the cards and the photographs were in hand and the latter were glued to the former, the cards were filled in with fictitious names. Father Benoît was careful to choose the most common names, 'to prevent,' as he said, 'that they would stick in the memory of anyone who happened to inspect the cards.' (Thus, before long, there was in Marseilles a large number of Jews called Jacques Dupont or Jean Duval—the French equivalents of John Smith or Jim Jones.) Baptismal certificates were then completed with the same names, and the four men were transformed into natives of Marseilles and the sons of good Catholic parents. Madame Leboucher was now ready to return to Rivesaltes.

It was a short trip, but, in those times of constantly policed trains, buses, and highways, it was a dangerous one. There would have been no way in which Fernande could have explained away the cards and certificates in her purse and, if caught, as she told Father Benoît, it would have been a very long time before she saw the light of day again. Luck was with her, however, and she was neither stopped nor searched on the way.

At Rivesaltes, Fernande handed over the cards to Ludwik, who, in turn, passed them, along with the baptismal certificates, to his four friends. The men immediately committed to memory, along with their new names, their new birthdays and the names of their new Christian parents. Once they were able to recite

that information without hesitation, Fernande briefed
them on the procedures outlined by Father Benoît. The
men, after their escape, were to go to Marseilles by public conveyance, being careful to avoid being conspicuous
in any way—such as by attempting to hitch-hike rather
than to take the train or bus, or by appearing reluctant
to show their ration cards if they were asked for identification. They were also provided with ready-made
explanations of the reasons why they, as residents of
Marseilles, had been in Rivesaltes. One was, for
instance, to pretend that he had been visiting his son,
who was a guard at the camp. Another was to be a
salesman who had been visiting the purchasing officer
at Rivesaltes on business. At the train station, the Gare
St. Charles, in Marseilles, special precautions were
also to be taken. A checkpoint for identification had
been set up at the exit of the station and, before being
allowed to leave, each passenger was required to
submit to a thorough examination of his papers. If
there was the slightest irregularity, the passenger was
taken aside and either questioned or held until the
police were satisfied that he was authorised to be in
Marseilles. Father Benoît, however, through his Resistance friends, had learned of a way to avoid this
scrutiny of documents. The men were instructed, upon
leaving the train, to go to the restaurant in the station
and to remain there for a while, until all of the passengers
had passed through the checkpoint. Then, they were
simply to walk through a door near the restaurant—an
unmarked door, unguarded, that led directly to the
street. From there, they were to make their way to
Father Benoît's convent, where they would be hidden

until a way could be found to get them into either Spain or Switzerland.

The plan, so painstakingly prepared, worked. All four men made their way, separately, to the convent in safety. Everyone heaved a sigh of relief, and began working on the next step: the escape from France.

The two logical places of refuge for Jews were the two neutral countries whose frontiers were relatively close to Marseilles: Spain, some two hundred miles to the southwest, and Switzerland, about the same distance to the north. It goes without saying that these borders were closely guarded, for it was common knowledge that the Unoccupied Zone of France was a gathering place for fugitives from the Gestapo, particularly for Jews and for escaped Allied prisoners of war. The Nazis were determined that none of these should pass over into neutral territory, and, since neither the Spanish nor the Swiss government was willing to return any fugitives who entered its territory, the Germans exercised particular care in the examination of passports at all crossing points. German thoroughness in that respect presented an obstacle, Father Benoît felt, that could not be easily overcome.

There was, however, a way to circumvent this difficulty, and that possibility lay in the Italian sector of France. Although the Italian zone of occupation was very small, the fifty-mile-wide 'demilitarised zone' ran the length of the Franco-Italian border, from Switzerland in the north to the Mediterranean in the south. At the southernmost point of this strip was the city of Nice, a city on which Mussolini had frustrated designs, and in which Father Benoît had friends.

The Italian troops and the Italian police in this sector were, it is true, allies of the Germans. They preserved, however, their own outlook toward life and toward their fellow human beings, and to the despair of their Teutonic ally, they brought a wholly Latin compassion to the administration of the demilitarised zone. Jews, though legally proscribed by Mussolini's earlier anti-Semitic laws, were, for the most part, allowed to come and go as they wished, and they lived comparatively normal lives wherever Italian troops and Italian police had jurisdiction over them. In consequence, the frontiers between that zone and Switzerland, and between it and Italy itself, were not wholly impassable to Jews. It was, therefore, to the Italian zone that Father Benoît determined that the escapees from Rivesaltes must go.

As a preliminary step, however, it was necessary to establish contacts in Nice. The refugees, when they arrived in that city, must be provided with shelter, and with the Italian documentation necessary for them to cross into either Switzerland or Italy. Father Benoît therefore went to Nice, where he called upon an old friend, a Jesuit, Father Brémont. Father Brémont was a long-time resident of the city. A distinguished man and a gregarious one, he knew everyone worth knowing in the vicinity. Among his acquaintance was a man named Angelo Donati, head of the Franco-Italian Bank, an influential and wealthy Italian Jew who had already expressed a willingness to use both his influence and his wealth on behalf of his persecuted co-religionists.

Father Brémont introduced Father Benoît to Donati, and the two found themselves in immediate sympathy with one another. A system was quickly devised for the accommodation of any refugees Father Benoît would send to Nice. With the co-operation of various Jewish charitable and religious organisations, which the Italians allowed to operate more or less openly, Donati was to find shelter, clothing, and funds for those in transit. With the help of friends in the Italian administration and police, he was to provide them with whatever documents were necessary for safe passage variously into Italy and Switzerland.

Father Benoît returned to Marseilles determined that his newly established 'underground railroad' would become operational as quickly as possible. The first four refugees, accordingly, were dispatched to Nice soon afterward, and it was learned a short time later that these initial 'passengers' had been well received there, and that, through the efforts of Donati and his collaborators, they had made their way safely into Spanish and Swiss territory. The experiment was, for all practical purposes, an unqualified success.

Thus encouraged, Father Benoît launched himself wholeheartedly into his work. 'Night and day,' Madame Leboucher recorded, 'Father Benoît was churning out forged identity cards and baptismal certificates, made out in the names of various non-existent Durands, Duponts, and Duvals. It was a time of great pressure from within and without, for we were still amateurs, unsure of ourselves and of our methods. A single false move, one indiscretion, would have brought the whole affair to the attention of the authorities, and—if we were lucky—we would then have spent the rest of the war in prison camps.'

Despite these dangers, for a time everything went well. While Father Benoît worked on documents in his convent, Madame Leboucher would travel to Rivesaltes, her purse and her clothes stuffed with ration cards and certificates of baptism. These were handed to Ludwik Nadelman, who distributed them among his fellow prisoners. The latter would leave the camp at the earliest possible moment, and following Father Benoît's method of avoiding scrutiny, arrive at the convent on the rue Croix-de-Regnier on the same day. There, they were hidden until Donati could be notified of their impending arrival in Nice. At the convent they were provided with decent clothing and with money for the trip, as well as whatever additional documentation might be necessary for their escape.

As weeks passed and more trips were made between Marseilles and Rivesaltes, and more and more escapees presented themselves at the convent, what, up to now, had been a minor problem began to assume major dimensions. The services provided to the refugees—food, clothing, etc.—required that a certain amount of money be available to Father Benoît. Various methods were adopted for finding the necessary funds—contributions from religious organisations, from Jewish charitable agencies, from various sympathetic friends—but money, though it became more plentiful, never matched the need for it. A new and regular source of funds was required.

At this point, Madame Leboucher, in addition to being Father Benoit's courier and liaison agent between Marseilles and Rivesaltes, also became a major source of funds. In Paris, before the war, she had been a fashion designer of some repute. She therefore hit upon the expedient of opening a fashion salon in Marseilles. It would provide a respectable 'front' for the escape operation and, in addition, it would bring in the money that was so badly needed. With the help of her employee, Victoire, Madame Leboucher had, in a very short time, converted her 'pigeon-house' apartment into a workshop where high-fashion creations began to take shape. To display her creations, she organised a fashion show at Marseilles's Grand Hotel, to which were invited the most important and wealthy people of the city. The show was a great success. The journalists were ecstatic. One of them, a M. Veran, wrote the next morning, 'The hit of the afternoon was the collection of hats, with its air of delicious and delicate fantasy.' He singled out particularly a creation of silver satin called 'Daily Bread,' which had been decorated with the figures of two peasants in the act of prayer—as in Millet's celebrated 'Angelus.'

This creation, which so ravished Veran, was to do a great deal for Father Benoît's organisation. It was bought at the show by an important customer, the Prince de Faucigny, for an exorbitant price. The sale of the hat itself would have been enough to satisfy the ordinary designer, but Madame Leboucher could not let go the opportunity to make an important point. 'Prince,' she said, 'the creation that you have bought is called 'Daily Bread' for two reasons. The first, of course, is an artistic reason. The second, however, is a reason of charity, for we are in a war in which many people lack their daily bread. You will be happy to know that you have contributed a substantial sum to the alleviation of that condition.' The entire profit from sales was turned over to Father Benoît and, thereafter, Madame Leboucher—now established as one of the city's most talented designers of high fashion—specialised, like Robin Hood, in taking from the rich and giving to the poor and the persecuted. It was, she felt, a most satisfying arrangement.

These additional funds came none too soon. The refugee escape operation had grown far beyond what had been originally foreseen. Father Benoît, ever sensitive to the injustices visited upon the Jews, had prevailed upon the Archbishop of Marseilles to appoint him 'spiritual director' to the two internment camps of the city. In that capacity, he was allowed to visit each camp once a week for the purpose of offering consolation and guidance to any of the internees who felt the need of such spiritual assistance. On the appointed day, under the eyes of the guards, he would go from one barracks to the next, talking to the men, advising them, and giving them news of the war. At the same time, he was also giving and obtaining information about relatives of the prisoners and, occasionally, arranging for the accommodation of a prisoner who planned to escape.

By this time, the influx of escapees to the Capuchin convent had reached such proportions that it had become difficult to avoid suspicion. Indeed, on several occasions, it was noticed that plain-clothes policemen or Gestapo agents were in the neighbourhood and were observing anyone who entered and left the convent. Nothing overt was done, however, until the police had evidence of what was taking place behind those austere walls. That time came when one of Father Benoît's protégés, a Jewish refugee, was arrested while attempting to cross the Spanish frontier. He was questioned by the Gestapo and, when he refused to reveal from whom he had received his forged papers, he was tortured. Finally, he broke, and gave Father Benoît's name.

From that time on, the Gestapo gave Father Benoît no rest. He was under constant surveillance and, in an attempt to find concrete evidence of his illegal activities, Gestapo agents time and time again, at all hours of the day and night, searched the convent thoroughly. Through some providential dispensation—almost miraculous, considering the number of refugees who came there daily—none of these searches turned up a shred of evidence, and the Gestapo always left empty-handed, forced to content themselves with threats and warnings of future action. As soon as the door had closed behind them, Father Benoît, with a Gallic shrug, would return to his work: his compiling of lists of names, his distributing of funds, his forging of cards and certificates.

Nonetheless, the danger was considerable that the Gestapo might, some day, come to the convent while Jewish refugees were quartered there. To avoid a possible catastrophe, Father Benoît was obliged to modify his method of operation. The refugees who came to the convent—many of whom had been referred to him by the Resistance, while others had simply heard that the Capuchin priest was a source of aid—were no longer hidden in the convent, but were distributed among friends of Father Benoît and among various Resistance families. These were Christians, both clergy-

men and laymen, Catholic and Protestant, who were
willing to run the risk of imprisonment if they were
caught harbouring Jews.

Another change, made necessary by the suspicions
of the Gestapo, was that the refugees no longer came to
the convent to obtain forged ration cards and baptismal
certificates. Instead, blank cards and signed baptismal
certificates were delivered by Madame Leboucher to
various Resistance agents, who then distributed them
among the group of refugees for whom they were
responsible. At the meeting place, Madame Leboucher
and the agent together filled out each card and certificate
according to the requirements specified by the agent,
for the date given on the baptismal certificate had, of
course, to correspond to the actual age and sex of the
recipient. These meeting places changed daily. One
day it might be in the back room of a florist's shop; the
next, at a lawyer's office; the next, in the office of a
beauty salon. The proprietors and employees in such
establishments were all Resistance agents, and the
variety of meeting places thus provided was unlimited.

One problem involved in this change was that of
transporting the blank documents and the official seal
of the Prefecture of Marseilles—for by now Father
Benoît was forging ration cards in such quantities that
it had seemed more convenient to have a copy of the seal
made (by a Resistance engraver) than to depend on a
supply of cards that already bore the seal. Madame
Leboucher, at the suggestion of one of her co-workers,
Antoine Zattara, solved the problem by constructing a
hatbox with a false bottom. Into the bottom of the box
went the documents and the seal, and the false bottom

was then secured. Into the top went the veils, scarves, pieces of felt, feathers, scissors, and threads, which are the stock in trade of the milliner. In addition, Madame Leboucher always carried in the box an assortment of head-scarves of various colours, for her own use. This latter was not a matter of vanity, but of caution. After conferring with Father Benoît in the morning, Fernande would choose a scarf of a certain colour according to the place where he had told her the meeting of the day was to take place. A blue one, for example, if the place designated was a restaurant; or a yellow one if it was a book shop. Then taking her hat box, she would go to a post office or to a bank and walk casually through the lobby. A Resistance agent stationed there would then determine, according to the colour of her scarf, where the 'contact' for the day was to be held, and he would notify the proper fellow agent. A while later, Fernande and the latter would meet in the appointed place.

Fernande was provided with a ready-made story in the event that she was ever questioned. 'I am a hat-maker; my husband works in Germany, and this is my only way of making a living. So, I always carry my materials with me. One can never tell when someone will want a hat made.' As proof of her story, she always carried in her purse a selection of newspaper clippings about her designs.

Such elaborate precautions seemed perhaps exaggerated, even at the time. As it happened, however, the opposite was true. On one occasion, the Gestapo raided a restaurant in which Fernande and her contact were meeting. Fortunately, they had not yet begun their 'business', and the cards, the certificates, and the forged seal were still safely in the bottom of the hatbox. Despite the fact that the restaurant was a perfectly orderly and respectable place, the Gestapo ordered everyone, Fernande included, to climb into the truck parked outside 'to be taken in for questioning.' Two German soldiers had been killed in the neighbourhood the night before, and the Gestapo hoped, by this hit-or-miss method of investigation, to turn up clues to the identity of the killers. Fernande, clutching her hatbox, did as she was told, and the group was driven to Gestapo headquarters, 425 rue du Paradis. Once there, the 'suspects' were deprived of all their personal possessions, and Fernande, with sinking heart, watched the hatbox disappear into another room. She was, of course, terrified for herself, but she was determined not to reveal anything of Father Benoît's operation even if she were tortured. If the cards and the seal were discovered, she would swear that she had stolen them in order to sell them on the black market. But then she remembered. The baptismal certificates! They had all been signed by Father Benoît! If the secret compartment in the box were discovered, there would be no way, no possible explanation, to prevent the priest's arrest.

The next few moments were a time of almost total panic. It was all over, Fernande thought. The Germans, thorough as they were, would discover the false bottom of the hatbox, and there would be no way to save herself from torture, and perhaps even death; and, infinitely worse, there would be no way to save Father Benoît. The organisation would collapse, and the hundreds of Jews who depended on it for their lives would be left alone and helpless. Fernande's very desperation, how-

ever, carried in itself the means to overcome despair.
Pushed to the verge of collapse by the realisation that,
at this critical moment, everything depended upon her
presence of mind, she felt a strange thing happen: 'I
suddenly felt something stirring within me. It grew,
filled me, took over my body and my mind. I felt a
surge of courage, born of desperation, and a determination to outsmart the Germans at any cost. They say that
an actress is great only if she knows how to play upon
the emotions of her audience. I told myself that I had
nothing to lose and everything to gain. I would lie
outrageously, flirt—anything. But I would get out of
this alive, and with Father Benoît's secrets safe. I was
absolutely and utterly convinced of that.'

By the time she was ushered into the interrogator's
office, Fernande had determined what role she would
play: that of the helpless and innocent maker of hats, a
poor, friendless woman struggling to make a decent
life for herself. She sat before her inquisitor's desk, a
tear running down her cheek, her voice small and
humble, heaving great Gallic sighs every few moments,
and told her story. Her husband was working in Germany, where, as he wrote, he was well paid and highly
thought of. Soon, he would be able to send her money.
But in the meantime, she had not a franc to her name,
the landlord hounding her for the rent, and her debtors
giving her not a moment's peace. And to make matters
worse, here she was, sitting in Gestapo headquarters—
an innocent working girl, picked up for no reason at all
—when she should be out delivering a hat to a customer.
At this point, she allowed herself a few demure
sobs.

The Gestapo officer, a young lieutenant, was obviously ill at ease. He tried to reassure Fernande, telling
her that she had only been brought in for questioning,
and that if she had done nothing then she would surely
be allowed to go.

This, however, only brought a fresh flood of tears.
'Ah, how easy it is for you to say. But you don't know.
If I do not deliver the hat today, I will be thrown out of
my apartment. I will have no money for food. And I am
alone. My poor husband, working night and day in
Germany, all for the glory of the Reich, and not knowing that in Marseilles his wife is about to be put out to
starve in the streets.

'Oh, sir. Question me, and you will see that I am
innocent. Here, look in my purse'—and she emptied it
onto the desk—'you see, there is nothing. It is true that
I had a hatbox, but they took it away. Ask for it and
look at it. It is nothing but materials for a hat. Please let
me have it back. It is all that I have for my work.'

The lieutenant, moved, and obviously half convinced
that no one so simple-minded could possibly be an
enemy of the Third Reich, had the box brought in.
Fernande herself seized it before he could reach it, and
began emptying it. 'You see, nothing but ribbons and
scarves and threads. Now, please, sir, let me take my box
and go. If you don't, then I will be ruined.'

The lieutenant was a German, but he was a man. 'Ah,
madame, what a pity that I am leaving Marseilles. You
need a friend, and it would give me much pleasure to see
you again. However—well, you are free to go. There is
certainly nothing suspicious about you. And'—he
smiled and winked—'I shall see that nothing of this

little adventure gets into the records. It will be as though you had never been here.'

Fernande backed out of the room, thanking him profusely. As soon as she was safely into the street, she hurried to the Capuchin convent. Father Benoît listened to her account of the day, and shook his head, smiling. 'Ah, Fernande,' he said. 'You live your life in the same way that you make your hats: by inspiration. An idea, and then a little decoration, a veil of mystery; and then, the touch of genius and, *voilà*—a unique creation. The poor lieutenant never had a chance.'

The pressures under which Madame Leboucher was now working were considerable. Occupying herself to the point of physical exhaustion with her now flourishing fashion business so as to provide funds to Father Benoît, delivering forged documents from one end of Marseilles to the other, travelling back and forth to Rivesaltes, and caring for the refugees who were now living in her apartment, she lived in a state of constant fear for her husband's life. There were times when, overwhelmed by depression and exhaustion, she gave in to terror and to the desire to abandon the entire operation to Father Benoît.

On one such occasion, she noted, she explained to Father Benoît her feelings, and concluded by saying that she no longer wished to be involved with refugees. 'He looked at me with a strange, intense, piercing expression. I felt that he could see into my soul. He said, in a low voice, "You cannot leave. This is your mission, your responsibility, and you must continue to the end. You must regain your courage. If you feel yourself begin to weaken, if you are afraid, then at that moment you must communicate with me through heaven!'' When he left, I laughed and laughed. "Through heaven," indeed! I was young, then. . . . Father Benoît was a learned man, a professor of theology. He had studied in depth the ways of God and of man. But I, my only dreams were of ribbons and laces, and my thoughts were of patterns. The books of theology had nothing in them for me; and they still do not. Nonetheless, Father Benoît had, I learned later, communicated to me through his words more than I could have learned in years of study. What I learned had to be learned instantly, by a sort of telepathic shorthand.'

The meaning of Father Benoît's mysterious words were made clear a few days later. Fernande had concealed in her apartment a half dozen Jewish refugees pending arrangement of their transportation to Nice. Late at night they heard a pounding and, at the same time, an order being shouted from somewhere in the building: 'Open up! It is the police!'

The police, with the Gestapo at their head, were in the building. It was one of the periodic and random searches, conducted from time to time, in which a number of buildings were picked out and searched for Jews or contraband.

It was obviously only a matter of moments before Madame Leboucher's apartment would be searched. The six refugees stood there terrified. Capture meant imprisonment and probably torture, or even death. There was no place to hide them, and no way for them to get out of the apartment except by the staircase—which, as they could hear, was by now filled with police.

Madame Leboucher was beside herself. What could

she do? The six refugees, for all their terror, were brave
men. 'Madame,' they pleaded, 'you must turn us over to
them. In that way, you will not be punished. If they
find us here and take you away, too, then what will become of the others, the ones who come to Marseilles
after us?'

But Madame Leboucher was in no mood for reason.
She simply could not bring herself to go into the hall-
way and summon the police, no matter how much that
seemed to be the solution. Father Benoît had entrusted
these men to her. 'It is your mission,' he had said. 'Your
responsibility.' She must save them somehow.

She wrote down later what she did. 'Nothing, it
seemed, could prevent the Germans from forcing their
way into my apartment and finding the Jews hidden
there. Hardly knowing what I was doing, I placed myself against the door, as though to block out the Germans by myself. There then seemed nothing to do but
pray, and I prayed a strange prayer: "Père Marie-
Benoît," I said, "I am calling you through heaven,
as you told me to do. Help me now!" Then I
waited.'

The noise in the building continued. Heavy boots
resounded through the halls. Doors were opened
roughly, and even more roughly slammed shut. The
sounds came nearer and nearer, and Fernande waited,
still barring the doorway, trembling, for the knock and
the order that she knew would mean the end of her
Jewish friends, and of herself as well. But nothing happened. The boots were at the next apartment, and
then, after a few minutes, they emerged and, somehow,
seemed to be descending the stairs. The police had

searched the house from top to bottom, from roof to cellar, every closet, cranny, and nook. Everywhere. Everywhere, that is, except Fernande Leboucher's apartment. For no earthly reason that she has ever been able to discover, they had by-passed her apartment door as though it had not existed.

Some time after that episode, Fernande wrote down her thoughts: 'Since that day, an almost supernatural strength was within me. The more dangerous the mission, the more exciting I found it. Between missions, however, it was as though I did not exist; or rather, I existed, but only in a limbo of inactivity. I could hardly move, think, or make decisions for myself. But when the time came for the next mission, I would hear an interior voice saying, "Go. Don't be afraid." And I went, and I was never afraid again—even though I not infrequently found myself in situations so precarious that only God's grace could have extricated me from them. From that moment to this, I never have doubted that a good God exists.'

The sequence of events in this instance was fortunate, for Fernande Leboucher was about to undergo an experience in which she would need all the courage and strength she had. Her next trip to Rivesaltes, which was scheduled for a few days after her narrow escape from the police, was to be her last. She arrived at the camp to find large signs posted around the area reading, 'Absolutely No Admittance.' The guards would not even discuss the possibility of admitting her, and they refused to summon the chaplain or to contact the commandant. Their orders, they said, were to admit no one, under any pretext whatever.

It happened, however, that the village of Rivesaltes was in the Prefecture of Perpignan, a city in which Father Benoît had friends. One of these friends, a worker in the Resistance, was an official of the prefecture, which had jurisdiction over the camp at Rivesaltes. Fernande therefore made her way to Perpignan, where she explained her mission to the Resistance agent. He issued her a special pass to the camp, but warned her that the camp was closed to outsiders because of the imminence of mass deportations to Germany. Finally, with evident reluctance, he showed her a copy of the list of those who were to be deported. Her husband's name was on it.

She returned immediately to the camp, where, despite her pass, she was told that she could see Ludwik for no more than ten minutes. It was time enough to hand over to him the half-dozen ration cards and baptismal certificates she had brought, and to recall to him, in the most urgent terms, his promise: that he would use his own card to escape when deportation had become imminent. And then she told him of the list. He quickly agreed to escape that very night, and they made plans to meet outside the camp. They were interrupted by the guard, who told Fernande that she must leave. As she walked back to the main gate from the barracks, she saw a group of men being marched in double file, their hands over their heads. Several SS soldiers were herding the men along, striking them with rifle butts on their heads, shoulders, and backs, toward a convoy of trucks that she could see parked at a distance. Some of the men were knocked down by the guards and she saw them fall, bloody, to the ground. The men were, she learned later,

the first group to be taken in the massive deportation.

Ludwik's escape that night went as planned. He and
several others made their way without incident to the
unguarded service road and simply walked out of the
camp. Then they separated to avoid being conspicuous.
Ludwik and Fernande met, as planned, in Rivesaltes.
From there, at the highway, they took a bus to Perpignan, and then a first-class compartment on the train to
Marseilles. Father Benoît had strongly advised his
protégés always to travel first class, for the reason that
no one, the police least of all, expected fugitives to do
so. As soon as the train had pulled out of Perpignan,
they heard the police in the corridors, checking, as
always, the passes and identification of all passengers.
As the voices drew nearer, Ludwik became visibly more
nervous; though he had his ration card, there was always
the possibility that the police would find it odd that he
had no passport, no working papers, no pass. Fernande,
however, was by now accustomed to danger, and she
made use of a simple ruse. She closed the curtains to
their compartment and went out into the corridor of the
coach, closing the door behind her and leaving Ludwik
alone in the darkness. Then, standing alone outside the
door, she calmly lit a cigarette and watched the police
approach.

When they had reached her, she smiled, handed them
her papers—which she had been careful to ascertain
were in perfect order—and, as they looked through
them, made small talk concerning the weather, the war,
and so forth.

'Is this your compartment, madame?'

'Yes, of course.'

'But why have you closed the curtains? Is there another passenger there?'

'No, of course not. I was waiting for you to inspect my papers, and I came out into the corridor to have a cigarette before going to sleep. I am absolutely exhausted, as you can probably see. I closed the curtains so that, as soon as you have finished, I can sleep undisturbed until we reach Marseilles. A woman travelling alone, you know——these are troubled times, *messieurs*. A woman cannot be too careful.' She smiled beguilingly.

The policemen smiled back, touched their caps in a salute, and moved on to the next compartment. How they could bring themselves to accept her transparent explanation remains a mystery, but accept it they did, and Ludwik was safe, at least until Marseilles had been reached. In the station there, the couple, following the system that Father Benoît had devised, ate a meal at the restaurant and then quickly walked through the hidden door into the street.

They went directly to the convent on the rue Croix-de-Regnier, where Father Benoît, who was expecting Fernande alone, was astonished to see Ludwik, whom, of course, he had never met. Fernande quickly explained the situation, and the three were soon deep in discussion about how Ludwik was to be hidden. The 'pigeon-house' apartment was quickly discarded as a possibility because of the likelihood of a police search similar to the one that had occurred only a few days before. Father Benoît suggested that Ludwik stay at the convent itself, where, he explained, he could be dressed in the habit of a friar. Thus disguised, he would be comparatively safe until some means could be devised to get him out of the country. Fernande pointed out, however, that, given the frequency with which the police now visited the convent, the presence of a new friar—particularly of one who spoke French with a trace of a Slavic accent, and who, moreover, was largely unacquainted with the forms of Catholicism, let alone with those of the convent life—would be enough to awaken suspicion. Finally, Father Benoît reluctantly agreed to an alternate solution: Ludwik would be sent to a small boarding house operated by friends of his who, in the past, had willingly provided a place of concealment for refugees.

As chance would have it, they arrived to find that the rooms at the house were all occupied. The proprietors, however, already aware of Ludwik's situation, offered to put a small enclosed porch at his disposal until the next day, when it was expected that a room would be available. At this suggestion, Fernande was inexplicably filled with foreboding, and she attempted to persuade Ludwik either to return with her to the pigeon-house, or at least to go back to the Capuchin convent for the night. He refused, saying that by now his escape must have been discovered, and that his presence either in his wife's apartment or at the convent would endanger not only Fernande and Father Benoît, but also the entire escape system. His wife at length gave in, and she left to return to her apartment, unable to rid herself of the feeling that they were on the edge of catastrophe.

The next morning she awoke depressed and plagued by the same presentiment. Hurriedly she dressed and went to the boarding house, where, to her horror, she saw Ludwik in heated discussion with a man in the garden. The man was holding Ludwik's ration card in his hand and, in a loud voice, declaring that he was a Jewish scoundrel, and that there were ways of dealing with Jews. He then told Ludwik that he was under arrest, and that Ludwik was to remain at the boarding house until the man returned with the police.

As soon as the man had left, Ludwik explained that he had been engaged in an apparently harmless discussion with the man when, possibly alerted by Ludwik's accent, he had demanded Ludwik's papers and identified himself as a police inspector.

'But he cannot be an inspector!' Fernande said. 'Otherwise, he would have taken you himself to the police station. He is a *poulet*—a professional informer, and he has gone for the police so that he can claim the reward money.' (The Germans had offered a bounty for all Jews and other fugitives who were turned over to the police, and Marseilles, like any other city in peace or war, had its share of citizens who were supported by the police in exchange for information.)

By now, the proprietors of the boarding house had come up to Ludwik and Fernande. 'You must leave at once,' they urged. 'The police station is a good distance from here, and it will be at least a half hour before he will be back. That will give you enough time to get away.'

Ludwik Nadelman believed in spiritual resistance to evil, and this had accounted for his determination to remain in the camp of Rivesaltes so long as he could help others to escape. That conviction also dictated his decision now. 'No,' he said with perfect calm, 'I cannot. If I did, then you would be held responsible for my escape, and you would be made to suffer for it. How are we better than the Nazis, if we make others suffer for our own sake? I will not go.'

Father Benoît had once spoken to Fernande of Ludwik Nadelman as 'one of the spiritual élite, of those who are the true saints of our age: those who are willing to sacrifice themselves, even their lives, in order that others may live.' That quality came into play now. Ludwik listened, deathly pale but at peace with himself, to the pleas of his wife and the arguments of his hosts. To Fernande's tears and to the proprietors' persuasions alike, he answered simply, 'No, I cannot. It would be wrong.'

After a short while, the informer returned with a police agent, and Ludwik was led away silently between the two men.

Fernande, desolate, sought out Father Benoît again. The priest's advice, like that of her first visit, was that there was nothing to do but to wait. And so they waited. A few days later, a postcard arrived, informing them that Ludwik had been sent to a collection camp at Gurs, near Marseilles. Immediately, the two made plans. Ludwik, while waiting for the police to come, had repeatedly told Fernande, 'Don't worry. Wherever I am sent, we will continue our work.' Now, with Rivesaltes out of reach, the camp at Gurs would provide escapees for the underground railway.

Once again, armed with ration cards and baptismal certificates, Fernande began her weekly trips to a prison camp, and once again Ludwik, refusing to escape himself, distributed these papers among those who were scheduled for deportation. The arrangement could have continued indefinitely had not tragedy, in the form of chance, intervened.

On one trip to Gurs, with a particularly large consignment of forged documents, Fernande arrived too late to be admitted to the camp. She therefore spent the night in the town, intending to give the cards and certificates to Ludwik early the next morning. At dawn she was awakened by the passing of a convoy of heavy trucks under her window. Again, she had a presentiment of disaster. Hurriedly she made her way to the camp and asked to speak with Ludwik. Instead of Ludwik, however, a friend of his, a fellow prisoner, came to the visitors' room. His face lined by an unspeakable sorrow, he told her what had happened. Ludwik had left his barracks before dawn to bring an identity card to a man who was about to be deported in a group of forty men. He had then guided the man to a place in the fence that he had discovered was passable and that was the regular route of escape for Ludwik's protégés. In the meanwhile, the men to be deported had been routed out of bed and lined up in the compound, where a head-count was conducted. To the consternation of the guards and the disgust of the German soldiers who were in charge of the operation, only thirty-nine were present. Ludwik's friend was to have been the fortieth. The Germans, cursing, ordered the guards to find a man, any man, to fill out their quota.

At that precise moment Ludwik crossed the compound on the way back to his barracks. 'That one,' a German shouted. 'Take him!' Ludwik was seized and hurled into one of the waiting trucks. He protested violently, but he was kept in the truck at gunpoint.

The administrator of the camp, a Frenchman, also protested, threatening to report this act of barbarism to the German authorities. The Nazis laughed. They were as insensitive to reason as they were to pity. 'All we know,' they answered, 'is that we are supposed to have forty men. We now have the forty, and we are ready to leave. Besides, what does it matter whom we take this time? Sooner or later, all of them will have to go!'

Somehow, Fernande returned to Marseilles. Father Benoît found her sitting in her apartment, staring vacantly at her patterns and sketches, overcome with grief and frustration. He had come to warn her that her pigeon-house was now under police surveillance night and day.

'I don't give a damn,' she said. 'Let them come. I only want to die.'

He looked at her in astonishment. Was this the woman he had thought so strong, so courageous?

'I am sorry, *mon père*,' she said. 'I simply can't continue. I am finished.'

'Fernande, this is no time for despair; above all, it is no time for self-pity. It will gain you nothing. You cannot give up. You must react, and react strongly, as Ludwik would want you to do. He would be the first to tell you that we must continue our work, regardless of personal sacrifice, and even tragedy.'

He continued in that vein, speaking for hours, warding off discouragement, pointing out that the war some day would be over and that Ludwik would then return. In the meantime, they must do everything that they could to get news of him. By the time he had finished,

Fernande had once again found the courage to agree to go on, and she was soon back at work.

A few days later Father Benoît managed, through friends in Paris, to learn that Ludwik had been imprisoned at Drancy, a few miles from Paris, preparatory to final deportation. He was to be there only a few days, and, if anything was to be done, it must be done quickly. Father Benoît immediately outlined a plan of action to Fernande that, precarious though it was, seemed to have some chance of success, and she left for Vichy the same day to put the first part of the plan into operation. In that city, the capital of the Unoccupied Zone of France, she spent two precious days attempting to see an official who might be able to help her, the Inspector General of Internment Camps in the South. Finally, she was admitted to his office, where she explained that she was French, a Catholic, the wife of Ludwik Nadelman. Ludwik, she continued, had been included by error in a group of Jews who were to be deported. The error, she asserted, was in thinking that Ludwik was Jewish, when in fact he was a convert to Catholicism. At this point, she produced from her purse a certificate of baptism, prepared by Father Benoît only three days before, which stated that Ludwik had been baptised in 1937.

The inspector general was perfectly willing to act on Madame Leboucher's behalf, and in a short time he put into her hands a release order for her husband, as well as a personal letter to the commandant of the Drancy camp calling his attention to Ludwik's case. But he added a warning note: 'You see that I, for my part, am eager to help you, but you must not make the mistake of believing that you will find the same attitude at Drancy. It is not impossible that you yourself, once you have been admitted into the camp, will not be allowed to leave.'

'I don't care. At least then I will be with my husband.'

'No, not even that. Women and men are housed in separate compounds. But I see that you are a determined woman, and I will not try to dissuade you. By all means, do what you must. But do not expect too much.'

His words were prophetic. At Drancy, Madame Leboucher presented the release order and the inspector general's letter to the camp commandant, who, after scrutinising both, courteously led her to the office of the administrator, where he left her after instructing the latter to do what he could for her.

The administrator, in turn, inspected the release order and then took a large folder from his desk. Opening it, he ran his finger down a page. Without a word, his finger fixed at one spot on that page, he motioned to Fernande to look. There was the name, Nadelman, Ludwik. And after it was scrawled the word 'deported'. She was too late. It was, she knew, the end. She would never again see Ludwik alive.* A sentence of deportation, as all Europe knew, was the equivalent of a death sentence. The deportee was sent to work in a German factory—very likely at one of the huge Krupp munitions plants—where he laboured for eighteen to twenty hours a day until, unable to go on, he was replaced by another deportee and sent to an extermination camp.

Fernande knew all of this, better than most people.

* Editor's note: Mme. Leboucher's fears were only too well founded. After the war she learned her husband had been sent to Auschwitz, where he suffered the fate of so many thousands in that inferno.

She had lived for months now with the dread of Ludwik's deportation like a stone in her heart. On the train
back to Marseilles, and now in her apartment, one
thought was present in her mind: now that that horrible
possibility had become reality, life was over for her, too.
All the work, the plans, the risks, it had all been for
nothing. No more would she see Ludwik's smile; no
more hear him laugh; no more feel his touch. To live
without him seemed unbearable; and death seemed ever
more welcome, a sleep that would put an end forever to
suffering and loneliness. It would be easy. So simple. A
few sleeping pills, a swallow of water; and then peace.

Victoire, Fernande's faithful employee, came to work
early the next morning. She had slept badly, and she
had wakened vaguely uneasy, for reasons that she could
not understand. Now, she found the door to the apartment locked, and there was no answer to her calls.
Seized with a sudden fear, she called the police, a
doctor, and Father Benoît. The police broke open the
door to find her unconscious on the couch.

When she regained consciousness in the hospital,
Father Benoît was seated next to her bed. She expected
sympathy, and condolence. Instead, the priest, not un-
schooled in the subtleties of female psychology, was in
a towering rage.

'How dare you?' he demanded. 'How dare you
attempt to take that which belongs to God alone? And
how dare you attempt to deprive our Jewish friends of
the only hope that they have of escape? You are essential
to our operation! We need you! How can you wish to
desert us, when Ludwik was willing to give his life for
our work? What would he say if he saw you now? He

would say, "Fernande, this is not the time for sorrow. It is a time to work harder than ever, to work so that others may be spared the sorrow that you feel.""

The shock of seeing Father Benoît in a rage, of hearing him raise his voice, of listening to the brutal truths that he spoke, had the desired effect. 'In a few days,' Madame Leboucher recalled later, 'I had thrown myself once more into our work. Father Benoît had been right. I was determined to sacrifice myself entirely to the rescue of my husband's people. Life now held no other interest for me.'

Although Madame Leboucher no longer had access to any internment camp, the flow of refugees and escapees into Marseilles did not diminish. Word had spread quickly that the Capuchin convent was a place where help and shelter could be found, and that a priest there was a true friend of the Jews. And so, they came by the dozens every week, crowding into the convent and into the various hiding places that had been devised in the city, and eventually slipping into the relative security of the Italian zone, or into Switzerland or Spain. The exodus had become so great that Joachim von Ribbentrop, the Nazi Foreign Minister, complained to Mussolini that, because of the inefficiency of the Italian troops in their zone, Eichmann's concentration camps were being deprived of thousands of Jews. The Italian dictator half-heartedly agreed to appoint a Commissioner of Jewish Affairs who, he asserted, would put order into the affairs of the demilitarised zone.

Shortly after, the new commissioner arrived in Nice. His name was Guido Lospinoso, and he held the rank of general in the Italian Army. By some incredible stroke of good fortune, Lospinoso was also a friend of Father Brémont, the distinguished Jesuit who had introduced Father Benoît to Donati and who had been instrumental in laying the groundwork for the escape of so many Jews. As soon as he had heard from Brémont, Father Benoît went to Nice, where he and the Jesuit secured an appointment with the new commissioner.

A long series of conferences followed. The exact nature of these exchanges has never been revealed, but, by the time Father Benoît returned to Marseilles, Commissioner Lospinoso had agreed not only to close his eyes to the steady stream of Jews from Marseilles into his sector, but also to co-operate in providing the refugees referred to him by Father Benoît with safe-conduct papers through the Italian zone. It was a coup of the first order. With both Donati and Lospinoso collaborating with him, Father Benoît was determined to accelerate markedly the speed with which Jews were being transported from Marseilles to safety.

The Gestapo, however, by now were desperate to put an end to an operation, of the existence of which they were certain. The Capuchin convent was watched twenty-four hours a day, as was Madame Leboucher's apartment. It was obviously only a matter of time before matters came to a head.

Fernande Leboucher was the first to feel the determination of the Nazis. Late one night, she and Victoire were working on sketches for a new collection—for the movement still depended to a large extent on income from this source—when there was a loud pounding on the door. Fernande, knowing in her heart what was about to happen, opened the door. Several Gestapo agents stood there.

'What do you want?' she demanded, with considerably more assurance than she felt.

The men answered not a word. Instead, they pushed past her into the apartment and stood looking around. Victoire watched them in visible terror. Suddenly one of the men wheeled upon her and, pointing his finger into her face, shouted: 'You! We are going to send you to prison until you rot!' Whereupon, Victoire fainted dead away.

Struggling to maintain an outward calm, while she was cold with fear within, Fernande said, 'She just learned this morning that her brother has been killed. Your uniforms must have frightened her.' And she went on, improvising—anything to keep them from asking questions. 'It is very sad for everyone, this war. I am sure that there are German women, too, who at this moment are mourning dead husbands, brothers, lovers.'

There was a moment of silence. Fernande could think of nothing more to say.

'We are not here to discuss German women. We are looking for a man, a certain priest of Marseilles, who calls himself Père Marie-Benoît. He is an enemy of the people. Do you know him?'

Fernande decided that a half-truth would be safer than an outright lie. It was likely that the Gestapo had seen her on her frequent visits to the convent. 'Of course. All Marseilles knows Père Marie-Benoît. He is the most able confessor and spiritual director that we have. I myself often go to his convent to ask his advice.

A holy man. So unworldly. How can he be an enemy of the people?'

'It is not your place to ask questions, but to answer them. Your "spiritual director," as you call him, is the head of a group of smugglers of Jews. Don't deny that you know all about it. Why don't you make things easy for yourself and tell us what you know.'

Fernande again made use of her recently discovered talent for the theatre. She laughed incredulously. 'Père Benoît? You must have the wrong man. It is impossible. Why, I am sure that he would not know a Jew if he saw one. He is a scholar, a professor of theology; those are his only interests.' She laughed again. '*Messieurs*. I think that someone has been pulling your leg. There may be people in Marseilles who smuggle Jews, as you say. Perhaps even priests. But if you think that Père Marie-Benoît is capable of such a terrible thing, then you are in for a rude awakening!'

Her superficial self-confidence and the lighthearted way in which she spoke seemed to shake their confidence. One of them, noticing a small crucifix around Victoire's neck—the poor girl had by now regained consciousness, and was sitting silently in a corner of the room—asked, 'Is she Catholic?'

'Of course. We are all Catholic in France. And you?'

'We are National Socialists, and patriots.'

'But that is a political party,' Fernande protested, 'not a religion. Since you were born before Hitler came to power, you must have been raised with some religious beliefs—or at least your parents must have belonged to one church or another.' Fernande had no idea where the conversation was going, nor any idea of how she was going to extricate herself from her rambling monologue. She only knew that, so long as they were talking, Père Benoît was safe. Suddenly, she had an inspiration.

Seizing a hat that she had recently designed, she said proudly, 'For me, this is my life.'

'Ah, an artist,' one of the Germans said. 'I myself wanted to be an actor before the war. But after all, "all the world is a stage."'

They talked on interminably. Whenever Father Benoît's name was mentioned, Fernande laughed and pretended that it was a joke; that the men were not looking for the priest at all, and that they had only used him as a pretext to gain admission to an apartment where they knew that 'two unattached ladies' were working alone. Finally, the Germans began to laugh too, and even timid Victoire, sitting in her corner, giggled and blushed prettily.

As they talked, it turned out that all of these young men had girl friends in Germany. Then, Fernande's inspiration was complete. 'Well, then,' she cried, 'take these hats. Each one of you, take one! Send them to your girl friends. They'll love them. This one is called "Paris"; this one, "Rue de la Paix"; that one, "l'Opera." Take them all!'

The Germans were completely disarmed, and Père Marie-Benoît was forgotten. The young would-be actor, with a Shakespearean sigh, began to read off the names of Fernande's creations: Thésée, Hippolyte, Démétrios, Obéron, Titania . . . 'For the moment,' Fernande recalled, 'he was no longer a proud National Socialist, a member of the dreaded Gestapo. He was the actor that he had wanted to become, and his humanity and sensitivity rose to the surface. Art had triumphed, and he was no longer a barbarian; in my pigeon-house, he had become a human being again. Our eyes met, and a message was exchanged. "I'll take care of this," he signalled. "Don't be afraid." And I knew that once again, by some miracle, I had escaped, and that, for the moment at least, Father Benoît was safe.'

But events were moving too rapidly for anyone to be safe. On November 7 of that year, 1942, only days after the Gestapo's visit to Fernande's apartment, it was announced that the Americans and the British had landed in North Africa. Hitler, alarmed at the possibility of further landings, perhaps in the South of France, and at the undependability of the Vichy government, ordered the German Army to move into the Unoccupied Zone on November 11. By the morning of November 12, the Nazis had formally occupied Marseilles. It was not until the morning that Pierre Laval, Premier of the Vichy government, had been informed by the German Foreign Minister that 'on account of information received during the night, Hitler has been obliged to proceed to the total occupation of the country.'

With the city now under the close supervision of the Germans, and the 'Jewish question' formally in the hands of the Gestapo rather than in those of the Vichy police, a reign of terror ensued. From November until February, Madame Leboucher recalls, 'It was as though we were living in hell. All that one heard was news of requisitions, manhunts, arrests, torture, deportations to the Nazi death camps, and executions.'

Gestapo pressures became so great that it seemed as

though the organisation that Father Benoît had so painstakingly created, which had saved hundreds and hundreds of lives, would either have to be dissolved or change its *modus operandi*. Warnings were received daily by the priest to the effect that he was on the 'wanted list' of the Gestapo chief, Müller, and that his arrest was only a matter of days, then of hours.

Madame Leboucher, meanwhile, was receiving the same sort of reports. In conference with Father Benoît, it was decided to abandon the pigeon-house. To have continued to operate there, would have surely meant that both of them would have ended up shortly in the Gestapo prison on the rue du Paradis.

Most important, however, was the problem of keeping Father Benoît out of the hands of the Nazis. It was not a matter of personal safety. The priest had never shown the slightest sign of fear at any time during his dangerous work. But he carried in his head an enormous quantity of information, for which the Gestapo would have given a great deal: the locations of dozens of hiding places in Marseilles and in Nice, where hundreds of Jews were concealed; the names of Resistance workers and sympathisers in the vicinity; the names of those who held forged identity cards and baptismal certificates; the names of important French and Italian officials who, either actively or passively, had co-operated in his work; and, of course, the names of those few close associates, Madame Leboucher at their head, who had been his most active and trusted collaborators. Who knew what tortures the Gestapo would be able to devise in order to extract such information? And who knew to what extent the human spirit, even one so strong as that of Father Benoît, could survive before breaking?

Father Benoit's Capuchin superiors provided the solution. They had never been in ignorance of what was afoot in Marseilles, or in the convent of rue Croix-de-Regnier. Indeed, the priest, as a devoted friar, would have hesitated before acting if he had not had at least the tacit consent of his superiors. Now, warned by their own sources of Father Benoît's danger, the superiors acted quickly. Father Benoît was ordered to leave Marseilles and to report to the Capuchin convent in Rome, where he was to become spiritual director and resume the teaching of theology. There was not a moment to be lost.

In preparation for his departure, all of the papers and equipment relating to the rescue operation were moved from the convent into two large trucks, which were then driven onto the grounds of a large house about twenty minutes by car from Marseilles. In the trucks were also Father Benoît, Madame Leboucher, and a few trusted collaborators. They were to set up a small rescue operation there, with the trucks as their 'office' and the house as their quarters. Father Benoît, though he had been compelled to leave Marseilles, had not received permission from the Italian government to travel to Rome. It was therefore necessary for him to remain in hiding for the time being. And what better way to occupy oneself, he thought, than in preparing for his project to continue after his departure? It turned out that he had left Marseilles not a day too soon, for the group heard later that only a short time after the trucks had pulled away from the convent, a Gestapo car had arrived. An officer descended and, waving an arrest order in the superior's face, had demanded that 'the criminal Marie-Benoît,' be turned over to him. 'Ah, monsieur,' the old priest had said. 'Alas! You will not find him here. He is gone, to Italy, to teach theology. These young priests today, they are never satisfied to remain in one place, you know.'

The estate onto which Father Benoît's group had moved comprised a considerable tract of heavily wooded land and a large house completely hidden from the road. It belonged to a family of the Resistance, who, some time earlier, had consented to take in and shelter a group of Father Benoît's Jewish refugees. Since the estate was well hidden and not too easily accessible, it seemed an ideal hiding place. They remained there for several weeks, until, early in June, Father Benoît received the papers necessary for the trip to Rome.

'Before leaving,' Madame Leboucher says, 'he gave us some last words of advice: to avoid Marseilles, as it was too dangerous, and to conduct our operations from the trucks, since they could be easily moved in the event of trouble. He made me promise to be brave always, and to keep him informed of what was happening.

'We escorted him as far as the platform of the train at Cannes. The whistle sounded, he boarded, and, as the train moved slowly away, we could see him, his gentle, kindly face at the window, his hand waving, until the train rounded a curve and he was lost to sight. He was gone, an ambassador, as it were, from the Jews of Europe to the City of the Popes.'

II
Italy

I

June 1943—September 1943: The Tragedy of Nice

FATHER Benoît, on his arrival in Italy, a country
very different from that which he had left only
three years before. In 1940, Fascism had been in its
heyday, and Benito Mussolini, rattling his sword and
strutting and posing before the world, was promising
the Italians a revival of the ancient glory of imperial
Rome. Much had happened in the interim, and, for
Italy at least, little of it was favourable. The Italian
armies had been so humiliated in an attempt to invade
Greece that the Germans had had to be called in as the
only means to avoid a total debacle. In Africa, the
Italian preference for surrender over combat had
become the subject of jokes that had crossed from the
lines of the Allies to those of the Germans and back
again. The Italian economy, under the strain of a war
for which it had not been prepared, was tottering.
Deserters were abandoning the armed forces by the
thousand every week and spreading disaffection and

defeatism among the people. The Allies, with North Africa virtually secure, were rumoured to be on the point of launching an invasion of Italy herself. The Italians themselves were disillusioned, restless, and, above all, weary. For more than two thousand years they had accumulated a firsthand knowledge of the futility of war. They had seen invaders come and go— Carthaginians, Ostrogoths, Visigoths, Vandals, Huns, Germans, Spaniards, Frenchmen, Austrians. War held few surprises for them, and no illusions. The sooner it was over, they reasoned, the better—on any terms, and no matter who the winners might be.

This spirit of public disaffection, even of disinterest, worked to the advantage of the Jews in Italy. Indeed, anti-Semitism, which in Nazi Germany was a corner-stone of national policy, in Italy had manifested itself chiefly in the subtle Latin guise of political expediency, a less malevolent variety of the disease, which was perhaps, and paradoxically, somewhat tempered by the traditional Catholic attitude of comparatively mild anti-Judaism. Mussolini himself, though eager to emulate his German counterpart in most respects, had long been torn between a public policy of Jewish suppression and a personal attitude that approached a grudging toleration. As early as 1908, he had observed that 'the subversion of morals is the chief occupation of the Jewish people. The people of Palestine [sic] were able to destroy their worldly enemies by destroying their codes of morality.' Yet, Mussolini was grateful for the fact that a considerable number of Jews were among the early adherents to his new Fascist party, and, when several of them were killed in a violent street demonstration, he publicly eulogised them as 'martyrs' and as men who were 'religious, poetic, and profound.' Nonetheless, a few months later, he had again reverted to an earlier posture and was deploring 'the Jewish character of Bolshevism.' In the following year, he executed another *volte-face* and bemoaned the treatment of Russian Jews by the Communists: 'Bolshevism is not, as many people seem to believe, a Jewish phenomenon; in fact, the contrary is true, and Bolshevism is leading to the complete ruin of the Jews of Eastern Europe.'

Mussolini's vacillation in this respect was very likely due to his well-known tendency to conduct public affairs by means of 'inspiration'—that is, by spur-of-the-moment decisions—rather than by the pursuance of a determined line of action. Whatever the cause, his inability to make up his mind continued throughout his flamboyant career. Shortly after his accession to power, his public attacks upon the Jews caused considerable unease in Italy, among both Jews and Christians; whereupon, the Duce hastened to give the Chief Rabbi of Rome a well-publicised assurance that 'the government of Italy, and Italian Fascism, have never intended to pursue, nor are they now pursuing, a policy of anti-Semitism.'

Despite such pronouncements, the dictator's sporadic outbursts continued and indeed grew so vehement that Pope Pius XI felt obliged to intervene by means of a papal decree of March 25, 1928, which reads in part: 'The Holy See, motivated by Christian charity, has always protected this people from unjust penalties, and, just as it condemns all hatred and conflict between nations, so too it condemns particularly and unreservedly that hatred, commonly called anti-Semitism, which is directed against that people who were once the chosen ones of God.'

Mussolini was not unaware of the enormous impact of papal pronouncements upon Italian public opinion, and, despite several serious clashes with the Vatican in the following few years, his official line was generally one of philo-Semitism. Late in 1935, for example, he wrote: 'Fascism does not require that Jews renounce their religious beliefs, their rituals, or their racial peculiarities. In fact, in Italy there exists no difference between Jew and Gentile in the political and social spheres. In a word, there is no "Jewish question" in Italy, and I have been careful to suppress anti-Semitic discrimination in the state wherever I found it.' Nor were his assurances reserved for sympathetic ears. In 1936, he told Hitler's ambassador, Dr. Hans Frank, that the Nazi persecutions of the Jews—which by now had reached the proportions of a world-wide scandal— were incomprehensible to him, because 'here I have neither anti-Semitism nor any quarrel with the Church. The Jews of Italy are simply good Italians, and even good Fascists.'

By the next year, however, Hitler's influence over the susceptible Italian dictator was increasing, and with it grew pressure for the adoption of an official attitude of anti-Semitism. At that time, official propaganda began to distinguish two species of Jews in Italy: 'Jewish Italians,' who belonged to the Fascist Party, and 'Italian Jews,' who were either non-members or anti-Fascists. Thereafter, 'Italian Jews' were increasingly discriminated against, and they were quietly deprived of any government positions that they held. Mussolini went so far as to appoint an official, a party member named Farinacci, to head his anti-Semitic programme of action, and it seemed that now a persecution would begin in earnest. Months passed, however, and, though there was a good deal of talk, there was little action. Mussolini, puzzled, did a bit of quiet investigation on his own, and was outraged to find that Farinacci, far from being a vigorous anti-Semite, had appointed a Jew, Joel Foa, as secretary of the anti-Semitic movement. The Duce was a man without humour, and he subjected Farinacci to a bitter tirade of reproach. 'It is no wonder,' he concluded, 'that foreigners refuse to take Italians seriously!'

By 'foreigners,' Mussolini no doubt meant the Germans. And he was right. Later that year, a group of Germans from the Nazi 'Racial Policy Bureau' settled in Italy and, shortly afterwards, Italy enacted her first racist laws, doubtless at Hitler's insistence.

The Church, though willing to condone a religious discrimination against the Jews, could never consent to racial discrimination. Immediately after the promulgation of the new laws, Pope Pius XI led the attack: 'The entire human race is but a single, universal race of men. There is no room in the world for "special" races. We must therefore demand to know why Italy in this respect should have felt the need to disgrace herself by imitating Germany.' Lest Mussolini be tempted to ignore this speech, delivered to Catholic students in Rome, Pius ordered that it be reproduced in full in the *Osservatore Romano*. This was a provocation that could not be overlooked, and Mussolini ordered his Foreign Minister to warn the Vatican that 'if the Vatican continues down this path, a clash is inevitable. The Duce now regards the racial question as fundamental to his policies.' The Vatican responded by denouncing racism as a horrendous error 'fundamentally opposed to Catholic doctrine.' Mussolini then adopted a different tack, warning the Jews of Italy in no uncertain terms that even more severe laws would be enacted unless they themselves managed to quiet 'these sudden and unexpected friends who are defending them from the pulpits.' Public opinion, however, was against Mussolini, and he knew it. King Victor Emmanuel, to whom Mussolini, at least in theory, was subject, expressed the feelings of his country well. During an interview that occurred in the midst of the Duce's altercation with the Vatican, the King told Mussolini, not once but three times, 'I feel an infinite pity for the Jewish people.' The third time, Mussolini was sufficiently exasperated to reply, somewhat sharply, 'Your Majesty, there are probably twenty thousand people in Italy who are moved by the fate of the Jews.' The King replied, no less sharply, 'If that is so, then I am one of those twenty thousand.' Count Ciano, who reported this exchange, noted that as a result of the King's words, the Duce was 'in a state of deep indignation.'

The Duce's own daughter, Edda, was even more outspoken than the King of Italy. In 1941, on a state visit to Berlin, she was subjected to an anti-Semitic harangue by Hitler. As the torrent of words showed no signs of abating she became visibly agitated, and finally she snapped at Hitler, interrupting him in mid-sentence: 'Oh, come now! Surely you cannot punish a man merely for having a Jewish grandmother!' There is no record of Hitler's response, but it can be imagined with what embarrassment Mussolini regarded his daughter's outburst.

If Mussolini's own flesh and blood refused to support his German-imposed policy of official anti-Semitism, he could hardly have expected the people of Italy to do so. And, indeed, he was not disappointed in that respect. Italian diplomats in the capitals of Europe did their best to protect Italian Jews resident in the countries to which they were accredited. The ambassador to Paris worked at this task so assiduously, and so openly, that the Germans had occasion to complain of him to a mortified Mussolini. German officers were constantly complaining that the Italian units alongside of which they were expected to fight were full of Jews 'and innumerable half-Jews.' Not illogically, one German expert on Jewish affairs concluded that 'we cannot therefore depend upon the Italian Army for any action, of whatever nature, against the Jews.'

Even Mussolini himself, despite his bluster and his determination to convince the Germans of 'the seriousness of the Italians,' could never bring himself wholeheartedly to implement the laws and the restrictions that had been promulgated at his insistence. When the Germans complained of Jews in the Italian Army, he turned a deaf ear. When they protested that Italian Jews all over Europe were being protected by the Duce's own ambassadors, he registered official indignation and then promptly forgot the matter. Sporadically —moved, probably, as much by a secret detestation of the Germans as by his native Italian recognition of the pointlessness of racism—he himself defended Italian Jews against the Germans, and it amused him occasionally to sabotage his own anti-Semitic legislation.

In the face of such national disinclination to the madness of anti-Semitism, the Germans could do little so long as Italy was an equal partner in the Axis, and the Jews fared better in Italy than they did in most of Europe. Pinchas Lapide, a contemporary Jewish historian of modern anti-Semitism, had declared, 'It was this Italian inability to harbour cold and systematic hatred as distinguished from brief outbursts of rage . . . this blessed incapacity, which made of Italy the foremost haven for Jewish refugees throughout the Hitler years and turned Italians into Nazi Europe's finest keepers of their Jewish brothers.'

This was an atmosphere in which Father Marie-Benoît felt immediately at home, and he immediately set to work to take advantage of it. As soon as he was settled into the Capuchin International College at 159 Via Sicilia, he took the initial steps in a plan that had long been close to his heart. As a beginning, he requested the superior-general of his order, an Italian who was known to be very sympathetic to the priest's efforts on behalf of the Jews, to arrange an audience for him with the Pope. This was no easy task. Pius XII, who had become Pope in 1939, an austere man and sometimes a forbidding one, was not a readily accessible pontiff even for heads of religious orders, much less for ordinary monks. Moreover, demands on the Pope's time had been multiplied beyond belief at this time of crisis, and private interviews were being kept to an absolute minimum. Nonetheless, the superior-general, through the good offices of friends in the Vatican, had been able to persuade the appropriate papal secretary that an interview between Father Benoît and Pope Pius would be of particular interest to the latter because of the Capuchin's priest's involvement with Jewish refugees. Accordingly, a private audience was fixed for July 16, 1943.

On that date, Father Benoît presented himself at the Apostolic Palace for the interview. The Pope received him kindly and listened with great interest to an account of the work that he had been doing in Marseilles. The priest then handed to Pius XII a memorandum that, as he explained to the Pope, detailed four points of great importance for the persecuted Jews of Europe, points on which the help of the Holy See was essential. After hearing a brief description of those points, the Pope promised to give the matter his personal attention, and dismissed the priest with a blessing for himself and his work.

The matters on which Father Marie-Benoît had solicited the Pope's help were as follows:

(1) The Holy See was asked to make use of its contacts, diplomatic and otherwise, within Germany to obtain news for their families of French Jews who had been deported to Germany. There had been a large number of such deportees, and nothing had been heard of most of them for a long time. In this respect, Father Benoît took the opportunity to describe to the Pope the methods

of deportation used in France, and also the conditions that—as the priest had learned through his own sources—prevailed in the Nazi concentration camps.

(2) The Pope was asked to use whatever influence he possessed to obtain humane treatment for Jews imprisoned in the concentration camps of occupied France. These subhuman conditions were described in some detail, and Father Benoît pointed out that not only Jews were detained there but also Catholic priests who had been apprehended in the act of helping refugee Jews. Such priests, the memorandum continued, willingly embraced the fate of their Jewish brothers, and some of them shared the 'ultimate solution' devised by the Nazis, shipment to Buchenwald and incineration in the infamous ovens there. 'These Catholic priests,' the SS guards scoffed, 'are nothing but Jews themselves. Into the ovens with them!'

(3) The Holy See was requested to intervene with the Spanish Government in order to aid in the repatriation of Spanish Jews being held in France. The Franco regime had promised to take the necessary steps, but the bureaucratic procedures were so lengthy and involved, Father Benoît pointed out, that these Spanish nationals were in imminent danger of deportation and death.

(4) The fourth point was that with which Father Benoît was most deeply concerned. Lenient

Italian policies in their zone of occupation in France had resulted in the concentration of as many as thirty thousand Jews there. Since it seemed only a matter of time before the Germans deprived the 'undependable Italians' of authority in that small sector of France, it seemed essential to Father Benoît that measures be taken to transfer those Jews from France to the relative safety of Italy. The Holy See was asked to apply whatever pressure was necessary on the Italian Government to bring about that transfer.

Pope Pius, as he had promised, set the papal Secretariat of State to work on the various projects outlined by Father Benoît. With respect to the first two points, however, the issue was disappointing. Relations between the Vatican and Berlin had deteriorated to such an extent that the Nazi government refused categorically to release to the Holy See any information regarding the concentration camps, either concerning conditions in them or with respect to the names or status of those imprisoned in them. Furthermore, a papal plea for humane treatment in the French camps was ignored, and did not even elicit the courtesy of an acknowledgement.

The third point, however, was brought to a more satisfactory conclusion. Two months after his audience with Pope Pius, Father Benoît received a communication from Cardinal Maglione of the Secretariat of State:

Dear and Reverend Father:
    Further to your memorandum to the Holy Father, dated July 15, 1943, the Holy See has been in contact with the Apostolic Nuncio to Madrid, and I

am pleased to inform you that some progress has been made in the direction indicated by you. According to a report received from the Nuncio, Monsignor Cicognani, the Spanish government has instructed its consulates in France to issue Spanish entry visas to all Jews of Spanish nationality, regardless of the political beliefs of the Jews concerned. The only requirement is that the latter be able to prove in some way that they are, in fact, of Spanish nationality —either by presenting proper means of identification, or because they are personally known to the consul, or because they are present at the consulate in circumstances which indicate that they are Spanish nationals; in the latter instance, such circumstances would be attendance at the celebration of a Spanish national holiday. In addition to the above-mentioned means of establishing Spanish nationality, the testimony of reliable witnesses will also be accepted as proof of such.

The Spanish government is, however, reluctant to issue, as you suggested, provisional, or temporary, passports, since there is always the possibility that such documents may fall into the wrong hands. You are urged, therefore, to concentrate your efforts on providing at least rudimentary evidence of the Spanish nationality of those who wish to avail themselves of the Spanish government's offer. You may rest assured that the Spanish border will be open to those who are able to present such evidence.

The Spanish government, moreover, has agreed to furnish, to those of the Spanish Jews who may wish to remain in France, documents attesting to the fact that they are under the jurisdiction of Spain. Such persons must, however, furnish some evidence, as explained above, of Spanish nationality.

Monsignor Cicognani adds that he has been assured by the government of Spain, that in deference to the wishes of the Holy See and in keeping with its own convictions in this matter, the conditions set forth above will be interpreted with ample latitude.

The Government of Generalissimo Franco was as good as its word. An official of the German Foreign Ministry recorded, on December 22, 1943: 'Diaz, the Secretary of the Spanish Embassy, visited me today and demanded that the arrest of Spanish Jews in France cease forthwith. The Spanish government is now determined to accept into Spain all Spanish Jews from the German-occupied territories.' Such was, in fact, the case. The Spanish government, instigated by the Holy See—which, in turn, had been moved to action by Father Marie-Benoît—extended this arrangement not only to the Spanish Jews living in France, but also to other countries such as Greece and Rumania.

With respect to the ticklish matter of what would constitute 'at least rudimentary' evidence of Spanish nationality, Father Benoît scored what was potentially his greatest coup. With the connivance of the Vatican and the Spanish government, he was appointed 'a disinterested third party' to judge, in cases of doubt, whether or not the evidence presented was sufficient. Despite this golden opportunity, however, Father Benoît was prevented from participating in the rescue operation. On July 25, Benito Mussolini had been forced to resign from the government, and he had been replaced by Marshal Pietro Badoglio, whom Hitler had once described as 'our most bitter enemy.' A radical change seemed at hand. It came shortly after the Allied invasion of the Italian mainland on September 3, 1943, when Italy surrendered unconditionally to the Allies, and Germany, in retaliation, took over control of all of Italy that was not occupied by the Allies. Since the German-occupied sector included Rome, Father Benoît was no longer able to communicate with his associates in France, and the planned rescue of Spanish Jews had to proceed without him. Moreover, Fernande Leboucher had by now been forced by circumstances to return to Paris and to her high-fashion salon.

But Father Benoît had done his work well. From France alone, some twenty-six hundred Jews crossed the Spanish frontier into safety. Thousands more came from other countries by means of the diplomatic door that Father Benoît had so adroitly opened, and still more thousands were released from concentration camps at the insistence of Franco's diplomatic representatives. Father Benoît's own description of this achievement is characterised by the priest's habitual modesty. After describing his interview with Pius XII and citing the letter from Cardinal Maglione, he concludes the episode by remarking simply, 'Unfortunately, by the time that this arrangement went into effect, it was no longer possible for me to communicate with France, and I was not able to help put these new measures into effect.' Despite that circumstance, it is primarily to Father Benoît—'to the ingenuity of that good Capuchin monk,' as one Jewish historian puts it—that the history of the times will attribute the saving of those thousands of lives.

The fourth point of Father Benoît's memorandum to Pope Pius XII, regarding the resettlement of the Jews resident in the Italian zone of France, likewise had to be modified in the light of subsequent events. The priest's original plan, as explained to the Holy Father, had been fairly simple in concept: to evacuate the Jews from that zone and bring them to Italy before the Nazis had the opportunity either to take over that area themselves, or at least to insist that the Italians apply in all their severity the 'Jewish statutes' enacted by the French (Vichy) government. At the time, that plan seemed entirely feasible, particularly if the Vatican were to prod the Italian Government in the right direction. Mussolini's Commissioner for Jewish Affairs in the Italian Zone of Occupation, Guido Lospinoso, as we have seen, had been entirely sympathetic, and even actively co-operative, with respect to Father Benoît's early operations in the area, and it was likely that he could be induced to sanction officially the evacuation of the Jews under his jurisdiction. Moreover, Mussolini himself had asked the Vatican's assistance in resisting strong German pressure to turn the Jews of the Italian sector over to the Gestapo. There was every reason to think, therefore, that a slight move on the part of the Vatican was all that was needed to ensure the proper decision on the part of the Italian government.

That move, however, was never to be executed. The Vatican was willing enough, and, at the instigation of Pius XII, the papal Secretariat of State had taken the initial steps, shortly after the priest's visit to Pius XII, to implement Father Benoît's plan. At the same time, Angelo Donati, the Jewish-Italian banker who had been Benoît's associate at Nice, was set to work at a less exalted level. On July 24, 1943, he visited Rome in order to open the question, through friends within the government, with the Italian Foreign Ministry. On that same evening Donati visited Father Benoît to report enthusiastically that their proposal had been well received by the Ministry, and that they might expect action, in some form, in the near future.

In the meantime, Donati and Benoît decided, it would be useful if they began finding places in northern Italy in which to settle the thousands of Jews who, if all went according to plan, would be coming into the country from southern France. So far the night of July 24. On July 25, when Benito Mussolini fell from power and a provisional government was formed under Marshal Badoglio, all was confusion in Rome, and no one knew what the policies of the new government might be. Donati, however, assured Father Benoît that the change in government—and the concomitant dissolution of the Fascist party—could only help their plan, and he returned to Nice full of hope for the future. On August 7, he wrote to Father Benoît that Badoglio's government seemed indeed sympathetic to the plan, and that, as the result of encouraging information received from his contacts within the Foreign Ministry, the Italian consul at Nice was then in the process of making an official presentation of the plan to the Ministry.

Moreover, the consul reported that the new Minister of Foreign Affairs, Giacomo Guariglia—the former

Italian ambassador in Paris whose protection of Jews was so open that Ribbentrop, the German Foreign Minister, had complained of him to Mussolini—had been much impressed by a report that Pius XII had expressed great interest in the plan. 'I do not thank you', Donati concluded, 'for all your efforts in this respect, for I know that you have undertaken this eminently Christian mission without wishing for, or expecting, either my own gratitude or that of my fellow Jews.'

By mid-August, Donati was again in Rome, where he and Father Benoît met to discuss their plans for the resettling of the Jewish refugees in northern Italy. Since it was expected that between eight and ten thousand people might take part in that great migration from the Italian zone alone, and that, in addition, some part of the approximately twenty thousand Jews who were hiding in other parts of southern France might be expected to cross the Italian frontier also, the problem of finding food, clothing, and lodging for them was not an easy one to solve.

Moreover, the Italian government would be able to give only very limited aid; it had few financial resources to fall back on for the financing of such irregular movement, and, furthermore, prudence required that it move cautiously in its own country. The Germans trusted Badoglio not at all, and they suspected him of attempting to negotiate a separate peace for Italy with the Allies. The slightest provocation on the part of the Italian government, therefore, might result in a German take-over of Italy—an event that would obviously spell the ruin not only of Italy, but also of Father Benoît's carefully laid plans, which presupposed a continuing policy of leniency toward Jews in that country.

Thrown virtually on their own resources, the two men planned in detail the distribution of the refugees among sympathetic Italian families and among convents, monasteries, parish houses, and religious institutions. In such a way, the problems of housing and food would be solved simultaneously, and, as an added advantage, it would not be necessary, for the most part, to separate members of families. Obviously, a considerable amount of money would still be needed for clothing, medicine, and so forth, but Benoît and Donati were confident that it could be found. Donati, after all, was a financier, and his talent for fund-raising was considerable; Father Benoît, though himself vowed to poverty, was also not without ability in that respect, and he felt sure that sufficient funds would be contributed by friends, by charitable organisations and by the Vatican.

When the two friends had settled matters to their satisfaction, their talk turned to other things. It was not until Donati was preparing to leave, some time later, that Father Benoît recalled a point that he had forgotten to mention. 'By the way, I meant to tell you earlier that a good friend of mine, Monsignor Hérisse, a Frenchman, is on good terms with most of the foreign diplomats accredited to the Holy See. He has offered to approach any of those representatives on our behalf if it would be helpful in our work, or even to introduce us to whomever we think it would be useful for us to know. It would be something to keep in mind. Such contacts might be very helpful later on.'

Angelo Donati was a man whom Father Benoît had

occasion often to describe as 'fertile in ideas.' That talent now came into play. 'Look, Father,' he said. 'Here we are, making elaborate plans to bring thousands of refugees into Italy and, we hope, to safety. It seems to be the only thing that we can do. But let's be realistic about it. What will happen to the Jews in Italy if the political situation or the military situation here changes? What if the rumours are true, and Badoglio is in fact trying to negotiate an armistice with the Allies? Surely we can't believe that the Germans will quietly pull out of Italy and let the country go its own way, or that they will allow the Italian government to turn Italy over to an American or British army of occupation. It would be suicide for the Germans to do that. What they would have to do in that event would be to take over the country—or at least to hold as much of it as they could. And you and I both know what they would do to any Jews that they found here. It would be Poland all over again—shootings *en masse*, deportations, Dachau and Buchenwald. We would not have saved my fellow Jews in that case; we would merely have delayed their execution, lured them out of their hiding places in southern France and left them out in the open here.'

'Yes, yes,' Father Benoît countered, 'we've considered all that. But what else is there? Surely you're not suggesting that we gamble with their lives by leaving them where they are?'

'No, of course not. But to bring them to Italy, which may well soon be as dangerous as France for Jews—perhaps there is another way, another place of safety.' He paused in thought. 'Tell me, does your friend, this monsignor, know either the British or the American representative at the Vatican?'

'As a matter of fact, he knows them both. Mr. Osborne, the British minister, and Mr. Taylor, President Roosevelt's personal representative, are both neighbours and special friends of his. But I don't see— wait, perhaps I am beginning to see—'

'You know what I am thinking. North Africa. It's completely in the hands of the Americans and the British now, and as safe as any place can be from the Nazis. We could set up facilities there for the refugees, with the help of the British and the Americans. Surely they couldn't refuse. If nothing else, public opinion would force them to agree.'

'I think you are right. We could ask Osborne and Taylor to propose the plan to their governments, explaining the extreme urgency of the situation. If they personally are in favour of it, it might just work; and, as you say, so far as the refugees themselves are concerned, North Africa would be a much safer place than Italy. However, even if we get the British and the American governments to agree—and that presupposes that we are able to persuade Osborne and Taylor— there will be one great difficulty.'

'Transportation?'

'Precisely. The way is almost clear now to bring the Jews into northern Italy. So far, so good. If they go to North Africa, they will have to leave from Italy, since the Germans control all other ports on this side of the Mediterranean. What we will have to work out between now and the time that we meet with the British and American representatives is the problem of how to get them from Italy to Africa. Or, perhaps, if the plan is approved, should we be thinking of transporting them directly from Nice, since that port is still in Italian hands, to Africa? There are advantages to both solutions and we will have to decide which one to adopt. In the meantime, I suggest we go on exactly as we have been, so that, if the new plan fails, we will have the old one to fall back on. I will speak to Monsignor Hérisse immediately, and ask him to arrange a meeting for us with Mr. Osborne and Mr. Taylor as soon as possible.'

As soon as Donati had left to return to Nice, Father Benoît went to see Monsignor Hérisse. The French prelate listened carefully to the monk's request and to his explanation for it. 'Yes, of course,' he said finally, 'I will do everything that I can to help. And I suspect that you will have no trouble in convincing either Mr. Osborne or Mr. Taylor. Today, I will call them both and ask them to receive you and Mr. Donati at the earliest possible moment.'

True to his promise, he telephoned Father Benoît later in the day to tell him that the American and British representatives to the Holy See would receive him and Donati in the following week. Benoît, elated at this first successful step in the new plan, immediately wrote to Donati at Nice asking that he arrange to be in Rome on the day specified for the appointment. Donati replied by return mail, confirming the date of the appointment and adding some significant news. In the few days that had passed since their conversation, Donati had spoken of the new plan to his friend the Italian consul at Nice, and the latter, with a speed that was miraculous in dealing with a bureaucratic government, had been able to obtain the assent of Foreign Minister Guariglia to the plan.

Not only that, he went on, but the Italian government, with unexpected magnanimity, had immediately suggested that it provide ships to transport the refugees from Nice to North Africa. The four ships suggested were converted passenger ships of the Italian line: the *Duilio, Giulio Cesare, Saturnia,* and *Vulcania*. Each ship was to make three voyages from Nice to Tunisia, Morocco, and Algeria; and on every crossing each of the ships was to transport approximately twenty-five hundred refugees. It was expected in that way that about thirty thousand Jews would be able to escape. The arrangements were therefore complete, Donati pointed out, except for the all-important consent of the Americans and the British. 'With God's help,' he concluded, 'we shall have that in short order.'

Donati's optimism was justifiable. As it turned out, however, he himself was not able to go to Rome for the interview with the Allied representatives, since the details of the arrangements to transport so many thousands of refugees required his presence in Nice. It was Father Benoît, therefore, who went alone to keep the appointment. He found Osborne and Taylor together at the latter's residence. Having gathered from Monsignor Hérisse's remarks that it was Father Benoît's purpose to present the same matter to them both, they had, as a courtesy to the priest, agreed to receive him together.

After the social amenities had been observed, Father Benoît plunged directly into the matter at hand. After describing first his original plan for receiving the refugee

Jews into Italy, he detailed the modifications that would make it possible to send them instead, if the British and American authorities consented, to safety in North Africa. The two diplomats listened politely and, in the immemorial style of diplomats, without giving any evidence of their personal feelings in the matter. As he concluded his appeal, Father Benoît decided that the importance of his mission was well worth a bit of undiplomatic candour.

'Gentlemen,' he said, 'that is the plan. It is a workable one, and it will save tens of thousands of lives. The Italian government has already agreed to it, as I pointed out, and has moreover agreed to furnish the necessary transportation. But it cannot be put into execution, obviously, without the permission of your two governments. If that permission is not forthcoming, and forthcoming very quickly, then one of two things must happen: either these Jews must remain in France, where they will also surely be seized by the Gestapo and suffer the same fate as their Polish and German brothers; or we shall follow through with our original proposal to bring as many of them as we can to Italy. It seems to us, however, that the latter can be only a temporary solution. We will be unable effectively to conceal so many thousands of people from the Germans if Italy should fall to them, and, in that case, they will die just as surely as though they had remained in France.

'In your hands, then, and in those of your respective governments, rests the fate, the lives and deaths, of tens of thousands of representatives of a people who have already suffered beyond description. I ask with all my heart that your governments allow these people to enter the areas of North Africa that you control. And I ask also that you make use of every means at your disposal to induce your governments to give that permission.'

When Father Benoît had concluded his appeal, the silence was broken by Myron Taylor. Speaking for himself and for Osborne, he stated that the plan seemed an effective and a sensible one, and that they would support it enthusiastically. They could not, however, give Father Benoît the permission that he required without first consulting their respective governments. They promised to do so immediately, and to use whatever influence they had to see that he received a satisfactory answer with the least possible delay.

The British representative confirmed the sentiments of his colleague, and Father Benoît left the American representative's residence with a reasonable hope that all would be brought to a satisfactory conclusion. He immediately communicated that feeling, by letter, to Angelo Donati at Nice. The latter, with a caution born of experience in dealing with governments, wrote back that, while he was overjoyed at Father Benoît's success in obtaining the support of Osborne and Taylor, and while he had every hope that the British and the Americans would endorse the plan, he felt, as did Father Benoît, that they must continue to follow through on the original plan. For that purpose, he suggested that it might be very helpful in bringing that plan to a rapid conclusion if Father Benoît were able to obtain another interview with Pius XII, in order to urge him to make known officially to the Italian government his support of the plan to bring the refugee Jews into northern Italy. 'Moreover,' he added, 'it would be a great help to us if the Pope should consent to express to the Italian Foreign Ministry his approval also of the measures being taken at the suggestion of the consul at Nice [i.e., for the transportation of Jews to North Africa].' Donati and Benoît had both discovered long before that, when human lives were at stake, it was always wise to 'hedge one's bets' in every available way.

Indeed, caution seemed the order of the day on all sides. Shortly after Father Benoît's interview with Messrs. Taylor and Osborne, the latter informed the priest that he had received a communication from the British government that was, the Minister was embarrassed to admit, not very encouraging. The British, according to that record, were 'giving serious consideration to the project,' and they would 'consult with Washington on the course to be adopted in that respect,' but they foresaw 'almost insurmountable difficulties, of a practical nature.' The difficulties, as it happened, were the result of a misunderstanding on the part of the British government, which had not grasped the fact that transportation for the refugees would be provided by the Italian government, and that the British themselves would not be called upon for ships. Père Benoît and Angelo Donati hastened to assure the British government, through Mr. Osborne, that all that was required of it was its official consent to the landing of the refugees in North Africa. They explained further that all expenses—'a rental of fifty-five hundred dollars a day for the ships themselves, to which must be added the cost of fuel and oil, as well as food, docking fees, etc.'—would be borne by Jewish-American charitable organisations, an arrangement that the influential and well-connected Mr. Donati had worked out. With these assurances in hand, Mr. Osborne felt that his government's hesitations would vanish, and he promised to expedite matters as much as he was able. In the meantime, there was nothing that anyone could do but wait.

And so they waited. Everything was ready. The ships, specially coated with a camouflage paint, were in port, already fuelled and staffed and ready to sail. The Jewish refugees had already assembled at Nice in numbers that Donati estimated at between forty and fifty thousand. They had been brought there through the good offices of the Italian government, which had provided some eighty large trucks, complete with armed police escort, to bring to the city all those who wished to go either to North Africa or, if that failed, to Italy. 'It was an agonising moment,' Donati recalled later, 'for in the event of the signing of an armistice between Italy and the Allies—which we all expected imminently— between forty and fifty thousand Jews would be thrown upon the tender mercies of the Gestapo. Indeed, the latter were already, as it were, pounding upon the gates of the city.' And yet, Washington and London seemed unable to bring themselves to give a simple 'yes' to the plan.

The first days of September passed, and still no answer was received from either government. Donati and Benoît, frantic with worry, used every means to obtain a decision. The banker attempted to contact, through neutral countries, influential friends in both countries—Lord Reading in Great Britain, and Dr. Chaim Weizmann, the president of the World Zionist

Organisation, in the United States. In a similar effort, Father Benoît persuaded Pius XII to make a strong personal appeal to the British and American governments 'to save the lives of these persecuted and unhappy people.' Both of these attempts were made by Donati and Benoît on September 7, but before either could bear fruit, time ran out. On September 8, the news of an armistice between Italy and the Allies was published. Immediately, German troops took control of the northern two thirds of Italy (the Allies were already in possession of the southern portion) and, at the same time, they swept over the Italian zone in southern France, where tens of thousands of homeless Jews still sat, waiting for the single word from Washington and London that was necessary to save their lives. The passage of a quarter of a century since that September 8 has not been able to eradicate the sorrow, not wholly free of bitterness, that filled the hearts on that day of everyone who had had a hand in the planned rescue. 'That day,' Father Benoît wrote later, 'saw the collapse of all our plans, with tragic consequences for the Jews who had been concentrated at Nice. The Gestapo took control of the city and arrested everyone on whom they could lay their hands. . . . The project had failed, simply because time ran out; and thus were condemned innumerable Jews, the salvation of whom had been our dearest wish.'

The tragedy of Nice was, perhaps, unavoidable. Father Benoît himself, one of the principals involved, is inclined to regard the event as such: 'It was a magnificent undertaking,' he wrote, 'which finally failed because there was not sufficient time for its realisation.' The historian, however, may be less charitably disposed than the priest, particularly in view of documents that have subsequently come to light regarding the attitudes of the British and American governments toward the resettlement of European Jews during World War II. In a volume of diplomatic documents from the year 1943 (published in 1963 by the U.S. State Department), one finds reprinted a memorandum from the British embassy in Washington expressing fear that the German government 'change over from a policy of extermination to one of extrusion, and aim, as they did before the war, at embarrassing other countries by flooding them with refugees.' This concern at the prospect of being inundated with Jews fleeing for their lives was shared to some degree by American official-dom. The same volume contains another memorandum, this one from the U.S. Chief of Staff, objecting rather vehemently to a proposal to move some four thousand Jewish refugees from Spain to camps in North Africa on the principle that such a solution 'would cause resentment on the part of the Arab population.'

Such attitudes, due perhaps more to ignorance of what was going on in Europe than to malice, seemed endemic among the Allies. In June 1944, for example, the infamous Eichmann suggested to the Allies, through an intermediary, a bizarre exchange: one million Jews, to be 'delivered' to North Africa, in return for ten thousand trucks. The reply of Lord Moyne, Deputy Minister of State for North Africa, was: 'What could we do with a million Jews? Where would we put them?' Also in 1944, to a proposal of Dr. Weizmann's for aid to Hungarian Jews, Mr. Churchill replied, through his chief private secretary: 'We have discussed this matter with the Soviets, and that's it'— meaning, simply, no. Such examples of practical indifference on the part of the Allies to the fate of European Jewry could be multiplied indefinitely from published documents; the above, however, are sufficient to give an insight into the reasons why the British and American governments were content to allow the Jews assembled at Nice through the efforts of Father Benoît and Mr. Donati to fall into the hands of the Nazis. Raul Hilberg, a historian of the Jews of Europe during the war, sums up accurately the reasons for the failure of the Nice project and of other similar rescue attempts: 'Within the State Department, there was disinclination to undertake large-scale action. Within the Foreign Office, there was fear of large-scale success. And within Axis Europe, fewer and fewer Jews remained.'

In view of these disinclinations and these fears, it is perhaps more than coincidental that, as Dr. Chaim Weizmann put on record at the Nuremberg trials, 'Not before July 1944 did Auschwitz reach its full capacity for extermination, with all four crematories in action.'

Father Benoît fortunately had no way of knowing at the time that it had been more than the element of time that had militated against his plans. He accepted the failure, which he regarded as his own, with humility, but with a determination to make reparation for it by greater efforts for the Jews. 'This is not the time for sorrow. It is a time to work harder than ever,' he had once admonished Fernande Leboucher. Heeding his own advice, he now set to work with a vigour that made his previous activities seem comparatively limited.

2

September 1943—June 1944: Rome

Tʜᴇ tragedy of Nice, deplorable and needless
though it was, contained within itself the seeds of
salvation for some Jews. While large numbers of those
assembled in the port fell, as had been feared, into the
hands of the Gestapo and were transported to the death
camps in Germany, thousands of others were able to
escape, and went into hiding once more in southern
France. Of these, many were eventually able to make
their way into Italy, where the detestation of the population for the Germans, and the ubiquitous influence of
the Church, seemed to promise a haven more secure
than that offered by France. For, despite the brutal
efforts of the Nazis, who now exercised iron control over
all but the southern third of Italy, a rescue operation of
the Jews, of such proportions that it amounted to a
national conspiracy, had been organised.

At the head of this conspiracy, as the most influential
—and almost the sole—benevolent institution still

functioning effectively in Italy at that time, was the Roman Catholic Church, whose guiding genius was then Pope Pius XII. It is one of the ironies of history that this Pope, while roundly berated by a later generation for his 'inaction' in the face of German atrocities against the Jews, was more than anyone else of his time responsible for the fact that Italy became—in the words of a Jewish historian already cited (p. 114)—'the foremost haven for Jewish refugees,' and that the Italians were 'Europe's finest keepers of their Jewish brothers.' A separation section would be required to examine this anomaly in detail, but it would be worthwhile here to note general papal and ecclesiastical attitudes toward Jewish refugees in order to understand the milieu in which Father Benoît was to work after the fiasco at Nice.

It would not be a great exaggeration to state that there was hardly a convent, church, rectory, school, orphanage, or ecclesiastical institution of any size at all in northern Italy that did not harbour at least a few Jewish protégés. Chief among these refuges was the Vatican itself, and such Vatican territory as enjoyed extraterritorial immunity from German invasion. At the Pope's summer residence in the little town of Castel Gandolfo, on Lake Albano, a few miles from Rome, for example, there were some three thousand Jews hidden at one time. Several dozen were sheltered at the Pontifical Gregorian University in Rome. Ten more lived for months in the cellar of the Pontifical Biblical Institute, across the street from the University; the number accommodated at the Institute was small solely because the Institute itself is housed in a small building. The same pattern was followed throughout Rome, and almost every institution that was exempt from German jurisdiction was filled to overflowing with refugees. According to one Jewish-Italian authority, some one hundred and fifty-five of these 'exempt' convents and monasteries harboured a total of five thousand Jews throughout the German occupation—that is, from September 1943 to June 1944.

The Vatican itself at times contained more Jews than Christians, and paralegal means were found to protect Jews who could not be so accommodated. For example, there has existed for centuries an honorary institution of papal guards called the 'Palatine Guards', membership which confers, automatically, Vatican citizenship. Because of the unusual immunities and privileges such citizenship implies, the number of Palatine Guards has always been kept to a minimum. In 1942, for instance, there were only some three hundred members. Between 1942, when the Germans began to apply pressure on Mussolini to enforce the anti-Semitic laws, and the end of 1943, when the persecution was at its most intense, the Germans noted that the Palatine Guard had grown to four thousand members—all beyond the reach of the Gestapo. Their indignation knew no bounds when it was discovered that many hundreds of these papal guards were unbaptised Jews. At that point, fearing that Vatican citizenship might not be sufficient to protect the most desperately sought Jews among his guards, Pius XII ordered that some two hundred and fifty be quartered in the Vatican itself. Other expedients were similarly adopted to confer the precious Vatican citizenship. An eminent Jewish scholar was employed in the Vatican library, where he compiled for Pius a magnificent map of the Danube Valley; whereupon the Pope, in a sensitively ironic gesture, presented the map as a gift to Von Ribbentrop, the Nazi Foreign Minister. The occasion caused one Nazi newspaper to comment, 'We remember a time when popes appointed no Jews to their libraries, when Jews were considered as descendants of Christ-killers and were treated as such!'

The laymen of Italy followed the example of Pope, cardinals, bishops, priests, and monks. Public institutions sheltered Jews by disguising them as regular clients. In poorhouses, they were carefully tutored in the manners, speech, and attitudes of born indigents. In institutions for the insane and the mentally retarded, they learned to simulate mental disorders and feeble-mindedness—necessary accomplishments in the event of frequent Gestapo 'inspections' in search of Jews. In private homes, individual Jews—men, women, and children—were passed off as refugee-relatives from the south or, when their Italian was not sufficiently good to pass inspection, from Yugoslavia and Austria. To support these pretensions, means of identification were necessary, and floods of forged baptismal certificates, confirmation certificates, first-communion certificates, membership cards in pious societies, affidavits, and even ration cards and passports, poured from the churches, monasteries, and rectories of the land.

It has been estimated that, during those dangerous months from the autumn of 1943 through the spring of 1944, some forty to fifty thousand Jewish lives were saved by these means. Much of this was accomplished by the efforts of individuals who could shelter only one or two refugees at a time. Others, however—church-

men, particularly—had at their disposal means to do a
great deal more. Cardinal Boetto, Archbishop of
Genoa, for instance, concealed almost a thousand Jews
in his archdiocese, a feat equalled by Bishop Palatucci
of the Campagna. The Bishop of Assisi not only hid
over three hundred Jews, but also built a synagogue for
them in the cellar of the monastery founded by St.
Francis of Assisi. The Superior-General of the Salva-
torian Order, a German national named Pancras Pfeiffer
used his considerable influence among his countrymen
to rescue over four hundred Jews, many of whom had
already been arrested and sentenced to deportation; on
one occasion, he was able to save eight Jews who were
already standing against a stone wall, waiting to be executed by a firing squad. An American prelate employed
at the Vatican, one Monsignor O'Flaherty, saved hundreds more by organising a team of workers whose duty
it was to find food, clothing, and hiding places for Jews.
The headquarters for this service was in an unlikely
place: the ground floor of the home of the Holy Office,
an institution better known by its popular title of 'the
Inquisition.'

Such work was not undertaken lightly, or without
consideration of the consequences. Three factors, however, probably were decisive, though in varying proportions, in moving so many people to run such risks.
First, there was a thoroughly Italian contempt for the
Germans and their laws, a sentiment not peculiar to the
twentieth century but traceable, through a thousand
years of history, to the pretensions of the (Teutonic)
Holy Roman Empire. Second, there was an equally
Italian attitude of compassion toward the persecuted, a

sentiment that, moulded by the dictates of Christian
charity, has been a national characteristic for uncoun-
ted centuries. And, finally, there was the factor that
played a decisive role in moving the laity and clergy of
Christian Italy from emotion to action: obedience to the
spiritual authority of the Pope.

In 1942, when it seemed that the situation of the
Jews in Italy was becoming more and more precarious,
Pope Pius XII had caused to be circulated throughout
Italy a command addressed to all Christians, and particularly to the clergy, to the effect that every means
available must be employed to save as many lives as
possible. There was no doubt in the minds of even the
most guileless Italian cleric whose 'lives' the Pope was
referring to. And no one who had ever had anything to
do with Pope Pius, or who even knew him only by reputation, could have believed that he would permit dis-
obedience to this (or any other) papal instruction. The
Bishop of the Campagna, Palatucci, who, as mentioned
above, saved almost a thousand Jews from the Germans,
was asked in 1953 why he had risked his life for the
Jews. His reply, as reported in the Israeli press, was
that, while he was moved by Christian charity, he really
had had little choice in the matter 'because of Vatican
orders, issued in 1942, to save lives by all possible
means.'

The wholesale acts of defiance of German authority
that resulted from these factors did not always escape
detection by the Nazis, nor did their perpetrators
always act with impunity. Although the Germans, motivated by a residual respect for public opinion, did not
dare violate the extraterritorial privileges of papal en-

claves, they were thorough in their search for Jews elsewhere, and they were ruthless in punishing anyone caught in the act, or even suspected, of aiding Jews. In those circumstances, a clerical tonsure, the habit of a monk or nun, or even a prelate's scarlet robes, carried no immunity from arrest. And, indeed, dozens of laymen and clerics were apprehended and punished, many being sent to prison, and some being deported to Germany, where, alongside their Jewish brothers, they paid for their charity with their lives.

In the midst of all this activity, it could not be expected that Father Benoît would settle down quietly in his convent on the Via Sicilia. His duties in that institution, as spiritual director to the clerical students, were relatively light, a circumstance that had allowed him to devote considerable time to the project of evacuating the Jews at Nice to North Africa. Despite the failure of that project, he was not discouraged; rather, he recognised that failure on one hand required renewed effort on the other. It was therefore only a question of time before he was once more in the midst of things.

As it happened, the opportunity sought him out. At the moment when the news of the Italian armistice had broken, a large group of Jews were on a train en route from Grenoble to Nice, where they expected to be able to board one of the Italian ships for Africa. When they heard the news of the Italian capitulation, they realised at once that their situation was desperate. There seemed to be no solution to their dilemma, except to jump from the speeding train and attempt to hide out in the countryside. While they were discussing this, however, fate, in the form of a railway employee who was either a firm Christian or an incompetent signal-man, intervened. The refugees suddenly noticed that their train was quickly being switched from one track to another. Before any of them had had time to recover from their surprise at this unexpected manoeuvre, the train shot off in a new direction: toward the Italian frontier. No amount of questioning of trainmen could elicit the slightest bit of information as to the reason; indeed, although the train was now proceeding at breakneck speed along an unscheduled route, they were careful to pretend that nothing unusual had occurred. The mystery was, in fact, never solved, and to this day the leaders of the group, Aron Kaszterstein and Stéphane Schwamm, can offer no plausible explanation. In any case, sometime later, when the runaway train had pulled into the Turin terminal, a group of puzzled, somewhat fearful, but altogether thankful, Jews emerged.

Their relief, however, was tempered by the knowledge that Italy, too, was now German territory, and that, while the possibility of arrest had perhaps been postponed, it had not been altogether averted. Moreover, they were strangers in a foreign country, without papers, ration cards, or connections. Yet, several of the refugees in that group recalled that Père Marie-Benoît, who had been able to be of help to them at Marseilles, was now in Rome. Perhaps he would be able to help them now, they reasoned, as he had in the past.

With that thought in mind, the refugees made their way clandestinely to Rome—no easy feat in itself—where, not knowing the location of Father Benoît's convent, they reported first to the organisation known as DELASEM (*Delegazione per l' Assistenza dei Emigranti Ebrei*, or Jewish Emigrants' Aid Society)— an association for refugee relief that had operated more or less openly under the Italian Government, but that now, with the German occupation of Rome, was about to go underground. DELASEM, at the refugees' request, immediately notified Father Benoît of the situation, and then hid the group in an orphanage.

The priest lost no time in responding to the request for aid. He went to the orphanage the same day, and was overjoyed to see several of his old friends from Nice and Marseilles among those who had escaped from France and, at least temporarily, from the Germans. The orphanage was not, however, a safe hiding place, Father Benoît pointed out, for the presence of so many adults would undoubtedly arouse German suspicions. Some other place must be found.

Up to this time, Father Benoît's Jewish activities in Rome had been confined to planning, first, the immigration of French Jews into Italy, and then the evacuation from Nice. He had had few contacts in Rome with those actively engaged in Jewish rescue at, as it were, the grass-roots level. Consequently, he had little idea of how one went about concealing such a large group of people. A DELASEM official thereupon suggested that the group be broken up and that individuals then be billeted with families that, as he knew from past experience, were willing to run the risk of arrest—in return for a not inconsiderable sum of money. It seemed the quickest way to get the refugees into safe hiding, and Father Benoît agreed to this solution. DELA-SEM, knowing that neither the monk nor the refugees had financial resources, offered to supply the necessary funds. The plan was therefore adopted, and the refugees were carefully distributed throughout the city. Father Benoît visited them daily, and at the same time came to know several officials of DELASEM—acquaintanceships that were to prove useful to him for the future.

Despite the fact that his friends were now adequately concealed, Father Benoît was uneasy. What if one of the families with whom they were lodged became frightened and, after having taken the money, reported the presence of the Jews to the Gestapo? They were now required by law to do so, and, after all, they would be severely punished if they were caught with Jews in their homes. Benoît spoke to Settimo Sorani, the chief of DELASEM, of his fears, and together the pair decided on a course of preventive action. The Germans had left some control of the city in the hands of the Italian police, and there were several police officials who were known by Sorani to be sympathetic to DELASEM's activities. He and Father Benoît therefore went one day to police headquarters, where they spoke to the chief of the section responsible for foreigners living in Rome.

The official received them affably and, after an exchange of pleasantries he inquired how he might be of service.

Mr. Sorani spoke first. 'We have come, as you probably suspect, on a matter of refugees. There are certain friends of Father Benoît's who have only recently arrived in the city. Being strangers, they were not aware of the regulation that requires them to register with the police, and it would be—inconvenient—for them to do so now. Is it possible that there is a way for them to be excused from fulfilling this requirement?'

The police official, of course, knew precisely who these 'strangers' were, but neither by expression nor by voice did he betray the slightest surprise. Turning to Father Benoît, he asked, 'These friends of yours, Father, from where did they come?'

'From the Italian zone of France, shortly after the armistice. I knew them at Marseilles, while I was teaching there.'

'I see. And are you willing to vouch for them? I mean, do I have your assurance that they are honest people, of good character?'

'By all means.'

'Then I see no difficulty. If you will give me an idea of the general area of the city in which they are lodged, I will see that my men do not disturb them.'

With his mind set at ease on the score of the Italian police, Father Benoît a few days later turned his attention to another problem, that of ration cards. These cards were similar in function to those with which the priest had had experience in France. They were issued by the Italian government to every legal resident of the city, and they enabled the bearer not only to identify himself but also to buy food, clothing, and medicines. By the end of September, such cards had become a virtual necessity. The initial confusion that had attended the armistice and the German occupation had begun to dissipate, and the Germans were now in full control of the city. Their search for Jews had begun in earnest. Suspected homes were raided, institutions were 'inspected' from cellar to roof, and ordinary citizens were pulled off the streets into Gestapo headquarters, and questioned. Everywhere and at any time, one was liable to be stopped and ordered to identify oneself. In these circumstances, it became obvious to Father Benoît that his Jewish friends would have to be provided with some sort of official means of identification. Baptismal certificates were one possibility, but a sudden flood of them might well arouse the suspicions of the Gestapo. Ration cards, since they were the customary means of identification, and since they moreover served a dual purpose, would be far preferable. He therefore set to work to obtain ration cards at once.

It was a delicate problem. Inquiries had to be made with the utmost discretion, and leads had to be followed up cautiously. At first, his efforts led nowhere. Several informants proved either unreliable or mistaken, and, for a while, it seemed that what had been fairly simple at Marseilles was impossible in Rome. Then, one day, Father Benoît was referred to a man who, he was told, was an employee in a government bureau, the Foreign Immigrants' Service. His quest seemed at an end, for the man declared, after hearing Father Benoît's story, that he, for his part, was also a friend of the Jews, and a good Christian into the bargain, and that he would be happy to supply Father Benoît with as many cards as he needed—*gratis*, of course. Within a few days of this meeting, he delivered to Father Benoît several dozen cards, all signed by the proper official, stamped with the government seal, and decorated with the correct amount of tax stamps. Benoît received them with gratitude and, congratulating himself upon the ease with which these apparently legal cards had been obtained, he quickly distributed as many as were needed among his Jewish friends. The rest, he put aside for future needs, rejoicing at the thought that, for once, he would be able to distribute real ration cards to the needy, and not forgeries.

His complacency was quickly shattered. A telephone call from a friend at the Ministry of Police informed him that everyone found in possession of one of the ration cards was in imminent danger of arrest. It seems that the man who had provided the cards had been less than candid in his relations with Father Benoît. He was not a government employee, and his cards were not, as he had maintained, 'quite legal.' Instead, he had stolen the cards, the seals, and the stamps, and he had forged the signatures. The theft had been discovered, and, as the cards were all numbered, they would be easy to trace. Moreover, the friend reported, the police had been notified, and they were on the lookout for anyone who presented one of these cards as identification. And, as though that were not enough, the thief had been arrested, and, in his confession, he had named Father Marie-Benoît, Spiritual Director of the Capuchin College, as his accomplice.

Obviously, there was not a moment to lose. Father Benoît immediately presented himself once more at police headquarters and asked to see the official who had been so understanding a short time before with respect to the refugees. The man was away, he was told, and would not be back in the city for several days. Feeling that, if the police already had marked him for arrest, he had nothing more to lose, Father Benoît identified himself and asked to see any official in the department responsible for issuing ration cards to foreign residents. As chance would have it, the official to whom he was referred was, as Father Benoît said later, 'a man of understanding.' He showed only polite interest as the priest worked through a long and complicated explanation concerning the ration cards, and then asked, 'And you say that you believed this man to be an official of the government, and that the cards were perfectly legal?'

'Yes, naturally. Particularly when I saw that they contained all the proper seals, signatures, and stamps. It never occurred to me to doubt the man for a moment.'

'And he never asked you for money in exchange for the cards?'

'Never.'

'Very strange. Not that I doubt your word, Father. But you were not the only one to receive these stolen cards, and, in every other instance, the thief sold the cards—at a very stiff price. When he gave us a list of his "customers," he included your name along with the rest, and we naturally assumed that you were an accomplice, in the legal sense of the term. The others who received the cards, you see, obviously knew that they were stolen, or they would not have been willing to pay; and, even if they believed that the man really was an official of the government, they would then have been guilty of bribing him—also a crime. It puzzles me that he did not attempt to get money from you, but who knows why anyone does anything? Perhaps it was because you are a priest. Or it may be that he was moved by a momentary sentiment of altruism. Such things happen.'

'What shall I do, then?'

'So far as you are concerned, you need not worry. I will see that your name is removed from our list. But you understand that the cards cannot, in any circumstance, be used, since they are forged and, therefore, invalid. You must turn them in to me, every one of them'—and here he consulted his file and mentioned the number of cards that Father Benoît was known to have. It was an accurate estimate. 'I am sorry, but that is all that I can do.'

'I see. I understand, of course. And I am very grateful for your understanding. I will see that the cards are returned immediately.'

'I understand, too, Father,' the official said. 'I'm sure that you will be able to find a—let us say, a less detectable way of obtaining cards for your foreign friends. I understand that such things happen every day in this city, more or less miraculously.'

And so, the cards were collected and turned over to the police, and Father Benoît began looking around for a miraculous, or at least for a 'less detectable' source of supply. He had achieved no results when, a few days later, on September 26, the Jews of Rome faced a terrible crisis. In one of those bizarre 'deals' that the Gestapo occasionally offered, the local chief of Gestapo operations, General Kappler, informed Settimo Sorani that he was about to order the arrest of three hundred Roman Jews, to be held as 'hostages.' The word 'hostages' in the Nazi vocabulary meant simply that the three hundred Jews would be shot by firing squads—a meaning that did not escape Sorani. Unless DELA-SEM, Kappler continued, delivered 50 kilos—about

1600 troy ounces—of gold to him within thirty-six hours, he would be obliged to give the necessary order.

Sorani was in a panic. DELASEM had no funds to speak of—and certainly no gold. Their financial resources had been exhausted by the enormous influx of refugees into Rome, and even if they were able to raise the money there would be no time to buy that quantity of gold. Kappler obviously was either feathering his own nest and wished to line it with an element of stable value —which Italian *lire* were not—or he wished to place the Jews in a position from which they could not extricate themselves. Probably it was a combination of both factors, as subsequent events dictated.

Whatever Kappler's reason for the demand for ransom, it was absolutely necessary to supply the gold. There was no doubt that he had every intention of carrying out his threat. Sorani therefore met immediately with Father Benoît and with the Chief Rabbi of Rome, Israel Zolli, and explained the situation to them. It might be possible, he said, to find that much gold among the Jews of Rome—many of whom had been the proprietors of prosperous businesses—but time was extremely short, and there was no assurance that 50 kilos of gold could, in fact, be found. He and Rabbi Zolli would start the collection immediately. But did Father Benoît have any other suggestions?

'Yes. First, DELASEM and all its personnel must go underground immediately and remain there. You would surely be the first ones taken if Kappler should carry out his threat, and then who would care for the refugees?'

'But our files, our records, our lists of contacts,'

Sorani protested. 'Where can we find a place to hide them on such short notice?'

'I don't know—wait, I do know. In my convent. They'll be well hidden there, and you'll still have access to them. While you and Rabbi Zolli collect the gold, I will move everything myself. So it is settled?'

'Yes.'

'Now as to the gold,' the priest continued, 'the only thing that I suggest is that you ask the Vatican to help. I am sure that the Pope would be willing—it is, after all, only gold in exchange for lives. The man to see would be the papal treasurer—I don't know his name, but his official title is "Apostolic Datary."'

'Should you be the one to go?' Sorani asked.

'No,' Benoît answered, 'I think that Rabbi Zolli would have the best chance of prompt action. I am, after all, only one of ten thousand monks in Rome, and he is the Chief Rabbi.'

The aged rabbi therefore went to the Vatican immediately and, after having identified himself, asked to see the Apostolic Datary. The rabbi's dignity, and the urgency conveyed by his manner and his voice, gained him immediate admittance to the office of the papal treasurer. The interview was brief. Forty-five minutes later, Rabbi Zolli was leaving the Apostolic Palace, holding in his hand a written guarantee, signed by the papal treasurer, of 25 kilos of gold—the amount that Zolli had specified, since he felt he could raise the balance himself. The treasurer, a monsignor, had showed not the slightest hesitation in assuring the rabbi that the gold would be forthcoming; but, he explained, he would have to have the Pope's personal approval for so large an expenditure. At these words, the rabbi had teetered on the verge of despair; he had had business with the Vatican before, and the process of obtaining Pius XII's personal approval was usually a tortuously complicated one, requiring days and even weeks of patience. The treasurer, seeming not to notice the rabbi's discomfiture, then proceeded to act with the urgency and disregard of protocol that circumstances demanded. A telephone call was made, a hurried explanation, and then a short wait while the message was relayed to Pius XII. Finally, the monsignor had smiled and said, 'The Holy Father is pleased that you have come to us, and he instructs me that I am to turn over to you as much gold as you need. With it, he gives his blessing to you and to your people.'

In the meanwhile, Settimo Sorani had been hurriedly collecting gold—vessels, jewellery, coins, and even bullion—from affluent members of Rome's Jewish community. He was joined by Rabbi Zolli, and, by the end of the day they had, to their astonishment, gathered together slightly in excess of the required 50 kilos. The gold was promptly handed over to General Kappler, who received it in silence, and the papal guarantee was returned to the Vatican, unused, with the heartfelt thanks of Rabbi Zolli.

The sense of security that ensued lasted less than three weeks. On October 16, 1943, General Kappler, in a massive Gestapo raid that penetrated into all parts of the city, swept up almost two thousand Jews into his net, of whom almost all were immediately transported to Auschwitz and death. As catastrophic as the raid was, it was not as bad as Kappler had intended it to be.

His purpose, as he had announced, had been to make Rome *Judenrein*. There were, however, almost ten thousand Jews in the city at the time of the raid, of whom approximately two thousand were refugees. Some 80 per cent of this Jewish population escaped, although the Gestapo was determined to make a clean sweep. What had happened was that news of the raid had been 'leaked' from Gestapo headquarters, and for the two or three days prior to the sixteenth a massive effort of concealment was carried out. By the early morning of the sixteenth, some eight thousand Jews had been concealed throughout the religious houses of the city. Israel Zolli, the Chief Rabbi, explained later how this had come about: 'The Holy Father, hearing of what was about to happen, sent a hand-delivered letter of instructions to the bishops and religious superiors, ordering them to lift the enclosure from the convents and monasteries so that these institutions might become places of refuge for the Jews. . . . No commander in history ever had such an army at his disposal. Legions of priests set to work to find bread for the persecuted and passports for the refugees. The nuns formed canteens to provide for women refugees. Superiors of convents, unworldly women, bravely confront Gestapo officers who come to their parlours demanding victims.'

This sheltering of the entire Jewish population of Rome was not merely a temporary expedient, one to be abandoned as soon as General Kappler's men had completed the first phase of their roundup. As everyone in Rome knew, from the Pope to the *ragazzi* of the streets, the deportation of two thousand Jews to Germany's death camps marked merely the opening of a campaign of extermination that was to last until either the Germans had been driven from Rome or the last Jew had been packed into a wagon and shipped, like an animal, across the Alps to die. The only solution, obviously, was for the eight thousand surviving Jews of Rome—as well as any refugees who might now come to the city—to remain in hiding permanently, or at least until—as now seemed inevitable—the Allies had succeeded in liberating the city.

Such a solution, necessary though it was, involved problems on a scale beyond the previous efforts of Father Benoît and his associates. Hitherto, they had provided for only small groups of Jews at a time. Now, an indefinite supply of food, clothing, shelter, money, and documents would be required, for an indefinite period of time. Many of the religious institutions in which Jews were hidden were not, with all the goodwill in the world, equipped to do more than conceal Jews within their walls. The finding and necessarily illegal purchase of large quantities of food, clothing, and medicine, the providing of forged identity cards—all these were beyond the experience of the other-worldly monks and nuns in whose hands the fate of their Jewish protégés now rested. Almost immediately, some of these religious houses sought out the man who, as they all seemed to have heard, knew what was to be done: Father Marie-Benoît. So now, by late October, the Capuchin priest and his friends from DELASEM had the responsibility not merely for a few Jewish refugees from France, but for dozens of Italian and foreign Jews.

After the catastrophe of October 16, DELASEM

had disappeared from view, at least so far as the police and the Germans were concerned. In fact, however, it had merely gone underground, and from there it continued its operations. Its affairs were now conducted by a committee composed of Settimo Sorani, president; Giuseppe Levi, secretary; Aron Kaszterstein and Stéphane Schwamm, Father Benoît's two refugee friends from Marseilles; and Father Benoît himself, who had been persuaded by Sorani that he could be of the most help to the Jews by working through the organisation. The anomaly of a Capuchin priest serving on the governing board of a Jewish agency did not escape Father Benoît's superiors, but they gave their approval with good grace. Nor did it escape the eyes of the young theological students in Father Benoît's convent, among whom a rumour sprang up that their Spiritual Director and Professor of Hebrew was not only a friend of the Jews, but a Jew who had converted to Catholicism. Occasionally, the more daring among the students would ask the priest outright if he were indeed of Jewish birth, whereupon Father Benoît would only smile mysteriously, as though both amused and flattered by the question. Years afterward, one of the priests who had been at the Roman convent with Father Benoît cleared up what the students, at least, had regarded as a mystery. 'You see,' he explained, 'Father Marie-Benoît is not Jewish at all. But he could not have loved the Jews more if he had had only Jewish blood in his veins, and he devoted every ounce of his energy to their welfare.'

Shortly after Father Benoît's election to the DELA-SEM guiding committee, however, Settimo Sorani

was arrested on one pretext or another, and held in jail
for almost two weeks. He gave a pseudonym to the
police, and exhibited false identity papers to substantiate
it, and eventually he was released. But from that time
forward, he was a marked man, and it was no longer safe
for him to go out into the streets. Father Marie-Benoît
was thereupon elected president of D E L A S E M, and
became, in that capacity, the official representative of
Roman Jewry. With due modesty, Father Benoît
explains his election: 'I was the only committee member
was was sufficiently unknown in the city to be able to go
about freely—to the police, to the embassies, to the
various government offices. It was a case of Marie-
Benoît, or no one.'

With Father Benoît's election as president of
D E L A S E M began the most dangerous and—for a
man who believed wholeheartedly in what he was doing
—the most exhilarating and most satisfying phase of his
career. In the approximately nine months of his active
presidency, the committee cared for some four thousand
Jews—not counting, as Father Benoît said, 'those who
were only passing through.' That total was composed of
various 'categories' of Jews. These categories were
based upon the refugees' places of origin, and were as
follows: Jews from outside of Italy, whose numbers
increased daily until, by the time of the Allied liberation
in the summer of 1944, there were approximately
fifteen hundred of them in Rome; Italian Jews from the
north of Italy; and Roman Jews.

The reason for such administrative divisions was that
each category required services and documents that the
others did not. Roman Jews, for example, were often

natives of the city—in some cases their families had been there for centuries—and they were relatively sophisticated in their approach to concealment, in that they were virtually indistinguishable, when they chose to be, from other Roman citizens. Often they required little but a hiding place, a food-ration card, and a forged baptismal certificate to substantiate the Gentile pseudonym neatly printed on the ration card.

Jews who were natives of other parts of Italy were similarly inconspicuous, although, since they were usually refugees in every sense of the word, their needs included funds for food, clothing, and medicine in addition to ration cards and baptismal certificates. Refugees from abroad—from France, Yugoslavia, etc. —were a particular problem since, in addition to being Jewish, they were also obviously foreigners and therefore doubly suspect. Those in the latter category thus required not only all the services provided to the others, but in addition their place of refuge had to be particularly secure, so that the possibility for contact with the outside world could be kept at the absolute minimum. It would have been impossible, for instance, convincingly to disguise as a nun, in an Italian convent, an aged Yugoslav Jewess who spoke not a word of Italian and who had never in her life been inside a Catholic Church. Or to pass off as a brother in a French monastery a young Polish Jew who spoke only Yiddish in addition to the tongue of his native land.

The headquarters of DELASEM, after being wherever the committee members could meet inconspicuously, eventually and naturally established itself at 159 Via Sicilia—an arrangement to which the father

superior of the convent, and the Superior-General of the
Capuchin Order, willingly consented. It was a compromising situation for the convent and for the order
itself, for the Gestapo was everywhere and the discovery
by them of what was going on behind those austere
walls would have led to the most serious consequences
for everyone concerned. One or two of the Capuchin
fathers of the convent, accustomed to a quiet academic
routine, were seriously disturbed at the conversion of
their cloister into the chief terminal of an 'underground
railway,' and finally complained about it to the Superior-
General. That worthy priest, a whole-hearted supporter
of the work that Father Benoît was doing, did not mince
words; having absolute authority over every Capuchin
friar and Capuchin convent in the world, he did not
have to. 'This is none of your affair,' he said. 'You are
not to worry about it, or to complain about it. After all,
if worse should come to worst and Father Benoît's
activities are discovered, it is not you who will be sent
to prison with him. It is I who will go, for it is with my
authorisation that he is doing what he does.' Father
Benoît was quick to sympathise with the fears of his
rather timid confreres. 'After all,' he pointed out,
'directly across the street from us on the Via Sicilia was
the notorious Jaccarini prison, the place where the
Gestapo brought Italian partisans and resistance
fighters to torture information out of them. Frequently,
we saw trucks and cars pull up opposite our front door
and discharge groups of these unfortunate patriots, and
never did we see them leave again. It was not a situation
calculated to inspire courage in the hearts even of the
bravest men. There was probably not one of us in the

convent who did not, at one time or another, picture to himself a scene in which the Gestapo would lead him across the street through those fearsome doors, to a fate that one could only imagine.'

Despite such encouragement by his superiors, Father Benoît was always painfully aware that his activities were compromising to his order and perilous for those confreres of his who were assisting in his work. Yet, his conscience would not allow him to stop for that reason. His work, he felt, was necessary in order to save innocent human lives placed in danger by a system devoid of all moral authority; moreover, it was a work condoned, and even commanded, by the divine law of mercy, love, and justice as well as by the papal mandate 'to save lives by all possible means.' He could not, as a Christian and as a Catholic, do otherwise.

With the establishment of DELASEM on the Via Sicilia, a system of operation was worked out to cope with the basic problems of rescue work among Rome's Jews. These problems were the ones already encountered in both France and Rome: lodging, money (for food, clothing, medicine, and other necessities), and documents such as ration cards, passports, and baptismal certificates to establish and maintain a non-Jewish identity.

Lodging, or a hiding-place, of course was the first and most pressing need of all Jews in Rome, whether or not they were native Romans. It was also a critical problem for Father Benoît and DELASEM. By some miraculous 'grapevine,' there was hardly a refugee in Italy who did not know that, at 159 Via Sicilia, in Rome, there was an organisation that would gladly protect him from the Gestapo. And there was hardly a day between September 1943 and June 1944 that several Jews, in groups or individually, families and strangers, did not ask the brother porter at the convent's entrance to see Father Benoît. Often, the refugees did not know his name. They had heard only that there was a Catholic priest who had helped many Jews and who would help them, and they asked for 'the Father who takes care of the Jews' or, more frequently, for 'the Father of the Jews.'

Once the Jews were brought into the convent, they were interviewed by Father Benoît or, if he was absent, by one of the other committee members, and it was decided what sort of 'services' would be appropriate in each particular case. The refugees were then taken, sometimes by a monk from the convent, to one of DELASEM's 'distribution centres'. These were usually private homes or religious houses whose tenants knew precisely, at any given moment, how many more refugees such-and-such monastery, or residence, or home for the aged could accommodate, and which of these hiding places were more or less secure than others in the neighbourhood. Since the entire city had been divided into DELASEM 'districts,' and each district had its distribution centre, Father Benoît, with the aid of his trustworthy distribution chiefs, was always able to find accommodations for his protégés. The refugees were then turned over to the distribution chiefs, who led them to their hiding places and presented them to those who would care for them there.

Such elaborate precautions became increasingly necessary as time went on. The attention of the Gestapo had been attracted to the Capuchin convent by the continual coming and going of groups of laymen, some of whom were obviously strangers and foreigners. As often as possible, refugees were asked to use the side entrance, on the Via Buon Compagni ('Street of the Good Companions'), so as not to be noticed by the Gestapo agents headquartered directly across the Via Sicilia; but the traffic through the main entrance, at all hours of the day and night, was still considerable. Undoubtedly, the Capuchin's German neighbours noticed this, for one day a friend of Father Benoît's— an Italian who was employed as a clerk by the Germans —telephoned to warn him that the convent was under surveillance, and that Gestapo agents posing as Jews would soon try to arrest him. The priest, feeling that the agents could not arrest him on such flimsy evidence as they had, decided to remain and face whatever danger there was.

The opportunity came late at night, shortly afterwards. A pounding on the door shortly after midnight brought a bleary-eyed brother porter to the entrance, where he was confronted by two young, ragged, but obviously healthy, bronzed, and somewhat overfed men. Carefully instructed by Father Benoît, the brother greeted the men with the courtesy that the Capuchin Rule requires, and then inquired after their business.

'We—we are Jews,' one of them said, in rather too loud a voice for a Jewish refugee.

'Ah, then God's blessing upon you, my friends.'

'We need help,' said the other. 'We need passports.' His accent was indefinable, but his voice and tone were of a man accustomed to giving orders. And what Jew in Europe, the brother reasoned, had given orders for the past few years?

Assuming an attitude of puzzlement and sorrow, the porter replied, 'Ah, then you have come to the wrong place. You must be looking for the government offices, though I don't expect that they will be open this late at night. Nonetheless, I will give you directions. You must go down—'

'You old fool! We are not looking for government offices. We are looking for the priests who take care of Jews!'

'Oh, my friends, then you are indeed in the wrong place. What would we have to do with Jews? We are only poor monks who know nothing of such matters. I regret that I cannot help you, but I will ask the fathers to pray for you. Good night, and go with God.'

Whereupon he closed the door softly, as the Germans stared at him in disbelief. He stood there for a moment, half expecting the knocking to begin again, or a command to 'Open! In the name of the Third Reich!' to be shouted. But nothing happened. He heard the pair talking as they walked down the steps, using such words as the good brother had not heard since coming to the Capuchins many years before.

'Up to that time,' Father Benoît recalled later, 'it had not seemed to us that there was a great deal of danger involved. Since the convent enjoyed extraterritorial rights—as a pontifical college it was a papal enclave— we knew that the Gestapo would not act unless they were able to catch us red-handed. At least, that is what we thought. What had worried us most was that a group of Jews might show up, looking for help, at a time that

Gestapo agents were at our front door or in our parlour. That, in the very best of circumstances, would have been difficult to explain.'

Now, however, in view of this most recent Gestapo attempt at 'infiltration,' it was decided that the danger was greater than it had appeared to be, and that the convent was no longer the inviolable refuge that it had been thought. After this visit, therefore, it was agreed that the various 'offices' of DELASEM would have to be changed frequently so as to avoid detection. Thenceforth, the distribution centres were moved from place to place at frequent intervals, as were the various 'depots'—usually convents—where stores of clothing were kept. The most dangerous locale, of course, the convent of Father Benoît himself, could not be changed. To have done so, the DELASEM committee reasoned, might have endangered refugees who came looking for help, for if the headquarters kept moving from one address to another, then no stranger in the city would have known where to go.

The second problem that Father Benoît and his committee faced was that of finding sufficient funds to provide for their Jewish protégés and, occasionally, to offer a small bribe to some petty official for some favour or another. DELASEM had had in its treasury, when Rome was occupied by the Germans, some 5,000,000 *lire*—about £125,000. In order to prevent the Nazis from confiscating the money, the entire sum had been signed over to Cardinal Boetto, of Genoa. With papal authorisation, these funds had been made available to Father Benoît when the latter became president of DELASEM. Since the money obviously could not be deposited in a bank, an involved and dangerous procedure was followed in supplying Father Benoît with cash for his needs. Every two weeks or so, a trusted messenger was dispatched to Genoa with a letter from Father Benoît to Cardinal Boetto that detailed the financial needs of DELASEM for the specified period. The cardinal would then hand over the required amount, in cash, to the messenger, who, travelling by train, brought it back to Rome as inconspicuously as possible. This went on until December 1943, when, by an unusual concatenation of circumstances, disaster struck.

The messenger had been dispatched to Genoa with a letter authorising the cardinal to hand over to him the entire sum that was left of DELASEM funds. Father Benoît had learned, through friends at German headquarters, that the Gestapo knew of the sum on deposit with Boetto, and that they were determined, in one way or another, to seize this 'Jewish money.' It was decided, therefore, to transfer the entire sum, in cash, to Rome, where it would be concealed in the Capuchin convent— a safer place, in the circumstances, than a Genoese bank. The money, however, never arrived in Rome. The messenger had been watched closely and, as soon as he had attempted to board the train from Genoa to Rome with the money in his briefcase, he had been arrested. The money was seized, and the courier was taken to Gestapo headquarters for questioning. He had refused to talk, and indeed had managed to make a rather dramatic escape and thereafter to find his way into Switzerland. He was safe, therefore, and neither Father Benoît nor DELASEM had been entirely compromised. 'We

were left,' Father Benoît said, 'quite literally without a
lira to our name.'

The situation, obviously, was desperate, and desperate measures were called for. Perhaps, a committee
member suggested, funds could be obtained from
America—from the Joint American Distribution Committee, the same Jewish relief organisation that had
generously borne, at Angelo Donati's request, a large
share of the cost of the abortive evacuation from Nice.
It was agreed that the idea was worth trying, and that
the best means of approach to the committee was
through the British and American embassies. It was not
unlikely, someone suggested, with more insight than
charity, that these diplomats felt a twinge of guilt over
the tragedy at Nice, and that they would jump at the
opportunity to redeem themselves.

The representatives in question, of course, had been
in no way responsible for the outcome of that project;
they had, in fact, been wholly in favour of it, and had
done their utmost to incline their governments to the
same view. Nonetheless, the American and British
ambassadors indeed seemed eager to demonstrate the
goodwill of their respective governments, and Key
Pittman, who was Vatican representative Taylor's
assistant, immediately wired Washington asking that the
government pass on DELASEM's request to the
Joint American Distribution Committee. Then began
an apparently interminable period of waiting while
Washington tried to decide whether or not to become
involved in this matter. Finally, upon Mr. Pittman's
urging, the Committee was contacted and immediately
agreed to furnish the money. Within a day, word was

received by Father Benoît that the required amount had been transferred to London.

Mr. Osborne, the British minister at the Vatican, now came into the picture. After a series of exchanges with his government, he regretfully informed Father Benoît that the money, because of a peculiar set of British wartime regulations, could not leave Great Britain through any of the regular channels of commercial banking. It could not even be sent to Switzerland. The minister, however, knowing how desperate was DELASEM's situation, suggested an effective, and somewhat irregular, alternative. Perhaps Father Benoît could find, he said, some well-disposed—and well-financed—individuals in Rome who might be willing to advance money to DELASEM in return for his own, Mr. Osborne's, guarantee of whatever sums were advanced in this way. In the meantime, the minister would attempt to find some legal way of having the Joint American Distribution Committee's contribution released from England.

It turned out to be an excellent suggestion. Two generous contributors were quickly found, and, thanks to their generosity and to Mr. Osborne's goodwill and ingenuity, DELASEM was once more in business. The sum involved—twenty thousand dollars—was not a large one, considering the by now vast operations of DELASEM, but it was the amount that Father Benoît had computed to be necessary until other, less complicated, sources of income could be devised. At this point, the Vatican offered to supply whatever funds would be needed for Father Benoît's work. It is estimated that a total of some four million dollars was thus channelled from the Vatican to DELASEM—much of which came from the American Catholic Refugees Committee, an official Catholic collection and distribution agency whose funds were at the disposal of Pope Pius XII.

On a par with money and shelter as preoccupations of Father Benoît's DELASEM committee was the matter of identity documents for Jews. This problem became particularly acute when an ordinance was published declaring that a 'residency permit' would henceforth be necessary for each and every person living in Rome, and that, moreover, no permits would be issued after December 6. It was a particularly vexing requirement, intended, obviously, to make it impossible for anyone any longer to shelter Jews. The Gestapo had long been puzzled by the fact that while a steady flow of Jews was known to enter Rome every day, they all disappeared into thin air as soon as they set foot in the city. The residency permits promised to solve that riddle for them, for there was no really safe way to forge them. Each permit was numbered, gave the name of the resident, and specified the police precinct with which he was registered. One could not forge a permit, therefore, for a pseudonymous 'Giuseppe Albano,' without running a great risk that, if Giuseppe were arrested, a quick check with the local police would show not only that the card was forged, but that Giuseppe did not exist.

It was generally agreed that this new requirement foreboded a new and intensive effort to round up the Jews of Rome, and it was decided that there was no way about it other than to 'legalise' the existence of

Father Benoît's Jewish friends. One way to do this was to obtain the help of foreign diplomats in Rome. It happened that Settimo Sorani was on particularly good terms with an attaché at the Swiss embassy. This diplomat had, on occasion, been willing, at Sorani's request, to furnish 'letters of protection' to various Jews who had been in possession of valid, or valid-appearing, French identity cards. These letters declared that so-and-so, a Gentile of good repute, was under the protection of the Government of Switzerland—a declaration that the Germans, with a logic peculiar to themselves, were willing to respect. Soroni approached his friend, therefore, with the request that such letters be provided *en masse* to the Jews under DELASEM's protection.

The Swiss diplomat was not as horrified as one might have expected at this proposal. Still, he was the representative of a carefully neutral country, a country whose diplomats were effective in Nazi-occupied territories precisely because of that careful neutrality. There were, therefore, certain obstacles. The first was that, since the attaché would have to account to his government for every letter issued, each individual asking for a letter would have to identify himself satisfactorily. 'What sort of identification do your protégés have?' he asked.

Sorani showed him a card of the sort that DELASEM had been forging, a crudely printed, transparently falsified document that would have survived only the most hurried inspection by a well-disposed official. They were being produced in great quantities by an amateur printer of Father Benoît's acquaintance.

The diplomat was visibly embarrassed. 'Ah, you see,

my friend, this will not do at all, I'm afraid. With each letter I must testify that I am certain of the identity of the bearer; and I cannot do that when I am presented with such an inadequate forgery. What I must have is a legitimate, valid French identity card. Or, lacking that, I must have at least one that is apparently legitimate and valid. It is not, you understand, that I do not want to help your friends. It is that I cannot do so on the basis of a forged card that is obviously such. Perhaps there is some way to improve the quality of your efforts?'

'We will try,' Sorani promised.

Father Benoît began trying immediately. A short time before, he had unearthed, in one of the convent's storerooms, an ancient printing press, covered with dust and obviously forgotten for many years. Now the press was hauled out, cleaned and oiled, and installed in the basement of the convent. As luck would have it, a master printer was found among the refugees, and he was set to work. A sympathetic engraver was found who, at considerable risk to himself, undertook to make plates that duplicated the official French identity card, and to duplicate the official French seal. The result was a creditable card that would pass any examination except the most careful one—in which latter case a few misplaced accents, and the quality of the colours, would reveal it as a good, though slightly amateurish, forgery. The most difficult task was to find real tax stamps for the cards. When this proved impossible—for they had to be French stamps—Father Benoît experimented with ordinary French postage stamps. He had a few himself, and the rest he bought from philatelists. These stamps were then carefully disguised by black marks—

as though they had been enthusiastically cancelled by a tax official—and then glued on to the cards in the proper place.

'We must have been out of our minds to think that we could get away with it,' Father Benoît has remarked. But get away with it they did. The Swiss attaché examined the new cards carefully, and then he ordered two hundred of the letters of protection to be prepared and signed. Thus, two hundred French Jews, by virtue of these letters, were able to demand, and receive, residency permits.

This had worked out so well that Father Benoît was inspired to try it with representatives of the countries from which others of his friends had come. The Rumanian ambassador, M. Grigorcea, was approached, as was M. Szasz, the Hungarian consul. To each of them, Father Benoît made a desperate plea, and from each of them, 'in the name of God and of our common humanity,' he extracted hundreds of documents certifying that so-and-so was 'a citizen in good standing of Rumania' (or Hungary), and asking that the bearer be accorded every courtesy. Since both of those countries were, at the time, allies of Germany, these letters were particularly effective, and many hundreds of Hungarian and Rumanian Jews (as well as a few Polish ones) were accorded residency permits with no difficulty whatever.

Father Benoît's reputation as a forger of official documents may be gauged by the fact that he was approached at this time by the French consul at Rome, a M. Deboise, with the request that the priest supply French identity cards to a number of Jews whom the

consul was hiding in his own house. Father Benoît
burst out laughing. 'Yes, of course I will. But doesn't it
strike you as strange,' he asked, 'that you, the French
consul, should have to come to a Capuchin monastery
to ask for identity cards?'

Italian Jews, obviously, could not come under the
'protection' of foreign governments, and so something
else had to be worked out for them. Since they had all
been obliged to change their names, they required new
documents to be able to obtain their residency permits.
After a good deal of hurried negotiation, it was arranged
that members of the Italian resistance movement—
with which Father Benoît was in more or less constant
contact—would find the necessary cards. The documents arrived shortly thereafter, and they were—at
least to the unpractised eye—indistinguishable from
authentic ones. They may even have been authentic, in
which case they would have come from a resistance
worker within the government. In any case, they were
never questioned by anyone in authority, and Father
Benoît did not think it discreet to inquire too closely
into the resistance's methods or sources.

These cards, however, were available only in a limited
quantity, and there were not enough of them to give one
to everyone who was in need. When the supply was
exhausted, other kinds of documents were used, some
forged, some authentic, some stolen, some legitimate—
'anything that fell into our hands, in whatever way,'
Father Benoît said. Among such documents, for instance, were passports whose owners had died or had
reported the passports to be 'lost' so that a legal replacement could be obtained. Such passports were

altered—i.e., the bearer's photograph replaced, his description changed—to reflect the likeness of the new owner. Some of these alterations were expertly executed, and some were very clumsy indeed. Despite these latter, there was only one instance in which the bearer of a document—an outrageously forged identity card—was arrested. On that occasion, the man, terrified at the threat of being sent to a German concentration camp, confessed that Father Marie-Benoît had given him the card. A friend in the police department immediately warned Father Benoît of the situation, and the priest's superiors found that sudden and urgent business of the order required that he spend two weeks in Milan. The police came and questioned the monks in the convent, who, to a man, pretended outraged innocence, and the matter was dropped. Curiously, the man who was arrested and questioned was not suspected of being a Jew, but only of being in possession of a forged identity card, since the other forged documents in his possession at the time of his arrest were all accepted as authentic; he therefore escaped with a comparatively light sentence.

Shortly after Father Benoît's return from Milan, he had one of the narrowest escapes, and one of the most bizarre adventures, of his career. Ever since the Gestapo had tried unsuccessfully to pass two of their agents off as refugee Jews, they had increased their efforts to find evidence that the Capuchins in general, and Father Benoît in particular, were all involved in a 'Jewish conspiracy.' On one occasion, several young Jews, who had been promised their freedom in exchange for information, agreed to help the Gestapo find evidence that would incriminate the culprits. The Germans, estimating that the game was worth the candle, determined to raid the convent despite the fact that it was papal territory. The worst that could happen would be that the Vatican would protest—but by then they would have their man safely in prison. Fortunately, Father Benoît was 'tipped off' a few minutes before the raid, and, at his superior's orders, he slipped out of a side door of the convent.

The nearest safe hiding place was a convent of Capuchin sisters a few blocks away, on the Via Piemonte, and it was there that Father Benoît presented himself at two o'clock in the morning. He explained to the mother superior what had happened. That lady, made resourceful by years of coping with a houseful of women, lost no time in condolences. Turning to the sister porter, she whispered instructions, and then asked Father Benoît to follow her into the cloister. The next morning, the community of nuns was startled by the appearance among them of Father Benoît—his beard carefully shaved, his hands modestly hidden in voluminous sleeves, his eyes demurely cast down—clad in the habit of the sisters of the Capuchin Order. He remained in the convent for a week, until informed that it was safe for him to return to the Via Sicilia.

His informant's information had been accurate. Only moments after his departure, the Gestapo had arrived, and, over the protests of the father superior, they had searched the house from top to bottom. They got nothing for their pains. All incriminating evidence— the printing press, the records of DELASEM, stacks of forged documents—had been convincingly buried under huge piles of books in the basement. The expected protest from the Vatican followed, and then the expected apology from the Germans. Then the convent was left in peace for a while.

In the procuring of documents for his refugees, Father Benoît found food-ration cards to be the most troublesome item. Yet, these were an absolutely essential item. As Father Benoît remarked to his committee, 'Baptismal certificates and identity cards are all very well. But one can't eat a baptismal certificate or an identity card.' The possibility of forging ration cards was considered, and then discarded. The cards were impossibly complicated—intentionally so, probably—and they were closely inspected on every occasion. The only possibility, it was decided, was to attempt to obtain them legally.

Fortunately, one of the committee members, Stéphane Schwamm, was an acquaintance of the official in charge of ration cards for foreigners. He proposed that they explain their problem candidly to the official—a man named Charrier—and hope for the best. There was, he pointed out, nothing to lose, for there was no other solution. Schwamm and Father Benoît therefore went together to Charrier's office, where they explained to him frankly—but not too frankly—that they needed one hundred ration cards 'for a hundred refugees coming from France' who had not been able to register for residency permits before the December 6 deadline.

Charrier was a public official of considerable intelligence and judgment who loathed the Germans as much as anyone did. He was quick to deduce from Father Benoît's words exactly what the situation was and to give his tentative approval to the proposal. He pointed out, however, that it was not as simple a matter as they seemed to think. 'A hundred ration cards is a large amount. I cannot just hand them over to you without some official justification. For instance, you could bring me the identity cards of your friends; that would prove to me that they are bona fide residents of Rome, and therefore entitled to ration cards.'

Father Benoît and Schwamm exchanged looks of alarm, a reaction that did not escape Charrier.

'However,' he continued, 'let us assume, merely as a hypothesis, that your one hundred Frenchmen have lost their identity cards—as happens every day in these unsettled times. Then I would have to have some sort of testimonial from a reliable refugee organization that they are who they pretend to be. That, I think, would serve the purpose just as well. The testimonial, of course, would have to bear the official seal of some authority, as well as the signature of the head of that agency.'

'Ah,' Father Benoît sighed, 'it is so complicated.'

'On the contrary, Father,' Charrier countered. 'I should think that, as a churchman, it should be fairly easy for you to obtain corroboration from a responsible authority—perhaps even from the Vatican. Do you think I would dare question a testimonial from the Vatican?'

And so it went, until Charrier had indicated a complete course of conduct to Father Benoît and Schwamm. They returned to the convent and set to work immediately, writing the text for the testimonials. Then, on their small printing press, they ran off one hundred copies, each bearing an impressive letterhead: 'Committee for Refugee Assistance (provisional).' '"Provisional" is absolutely right,' Father Benoît commented, 'because the whole scheme can only work provided no one catches on to what this famous "Committee" really is.' The text itself followed closely what Charrier had suggested. 'It should sound official,' he had said. 'But be careful not to go into too much detail concerning either the organization or the person for whom you wish the card. Say simply that So-and-So is a French national, and that your organization—whatever you decide to call it—is responsible for regularizing his civil status. Remember that the most important thing is that the testimonial make a good impression on whoever reads it.'

Schwamm and Father Benoît inspected their handiwork carefully and decided that it met Charrier's specifications. The priest then signed each one carefully, adding, with a flourish, the title 'Executive Director.' All that was lacking now was 'the official seal of some authority,' and, accordingly, they went directly to the office of the Vicar of Rome, the cardinal responsible for the administration of the Pope's diocese of Rome. The Vicar of Rome—who at that time was Cardinal Micara—was then, as now, recognized by the Italian government as a civic official as well as an ecclesiastical one; the seal of this dual authority, Father Benoît felt, would do very nicely.

They were received at the Vicarage by a rather nervous monsignor, who, while he was sympathetic to their plight, hesitated to comply with their request. 'I simply don't know, Father,' he said. 'What you are

asking me to do is to swear, in the place of His Emin-
ence, that this committee of yours is a legally constituted
entity, and that you are officially responsible for the
persons named on these certificates. It seems to me that
this would compromise the Vicar—'

'One hundred Jewish lives, Monsignor,' Father
Benoît said quietly.

The monsignor sat in silence for a few seconds,
staring out of the window and drumming his fingers on
the desk. Then his face brightened. He had not risen
in the Church by being unimaginative. Seizing the
stack of certificates on his desk, he read the first one
over carefully, and then asked, 'Did you sign this
testimonial, Father Benoît?'

'I did. Why?'

'Good. Now, sign this.' He thrust a blank sheet of
paper before Father Benoît and indicated a pen on the
desk. Father Benoît signed.

The monsignor then examined the signature carefully and compared it to that on the bottom of the
testimonials. 'Yes, yes. It is the same,' he murmured.
Then, taking the pen himself, he began rapidly signing
the testimonials, embossing on each one the seal of the
Vicariate of Rome. 'You understand, Father, that all I
am doing is certifying that this is indeed your signature
on each one of these documents.'

'But—'

'Of course,' the monsignor continued, speaking
while he signed and sealed, 'if a third party, under-
standably ignorant of our intentions, should interpret
this seal and this signature in another sense—well, that
is not my problem.'

An hour later, Father Benoît was at the office of Mr. Charrier with the precious documents. The official inspected them carefully, and then showed them to his own superior. They declared themselves satisfied, and one hundred ration cards were issued promptly. Father Benoît distributed them among refugees who had arrived in Rome too late to be eligible for residency permits, for whom they served as unassailable evidence of identity.

The same methods were used to obtain cards for Jews from nations other than France, and they were modified only slightly, at Charrier's suggestion, in the case of Italian Jews. The latter were certified, by the Committee for Refugee Assistance (provisional), to be Italian nationals who had fled to their homeland from Ethiopia, Greece, Albania, etc., and whose papers had either been lost in the process or destroyed during the Allied bombing and invasion. The committee's function in their regard, according to the formula dictated by Charrier, was 'to regularize their civil status by obtaining, on their behalf, replacement of such necessary documents as have been lost or destroyed. . . .' By such paralegal methods, over thirteen hundred legal ration cards were obtained by Father Benoît for Jewish refugees in Rome.

It was a Herculean feat, particularly when one considers that it was practically impossible at that time for anyone who was not a citizen of Rome to obtain these cards; even German officers and soldiers stationed in the city were normally turned down when they applied for them. As a result of it, the Jews of Rome gradually disappeared by the thousands, and were replaced by thousands of Frenchmen, Greeks, Hungarians, Poles, Yugoslavs, Rumanians, Swiss, and returned Italian colonists.

So encouraging were these results that Father Benoît determined to try his hand at something that, up to now, had seemed beyond the realm of the possible: the procurement of residency permits. (These were cards, signed by the head of the local police, certifying that the bearer was a registered and duly authorized resident of the city of Rome.) He and Schwamm again approached their monsignor in the Vicariate of Rome, and again the prelate expressed his willingness to help them in the same way as before. Moreover, he introduced them to a friend of his, the secretary to the Quaestor of Rome. The Quaestor himself, to whom Father Benoît and Schwamm were presented by the secretary, was the man ultimately responsible for residency permits. Like Charrier, he stated that a certificate from the committee, so long as it bore the seal of the Vicar of Rome, was, to his mind, sufficient grounds for the issuance of a permit; and he added that he would instruct the police to honour such certificates. He cautioned, however, that the priest was not to send more than twenty refugees a day to the police precincts. More than that, and people might begin to ask questions.

For a while, all went well. Every day, a score of refugees of various nationalities, all armed with their ration cards and their testimonials from the Committee for Refugee Assistance (provisional), presented themselves at the police bureau and were issued their residency permits without trouble. Suddenly, when several hundred Jews had been processed in this way, the police refused any longer to honour the testimonials. In the manner of police the world over, they refused to give any reason for this stand, stating simply, and with finality, 'Regrettably, we are unable to comply with your request.'

Stéphane Schwamm came up with a solution. This committee member, fortified with a forged passport, forged identity card, legal ration card, and legal residency permit, had now become M. Bernard Lioré, French citizen, Christian, and patriot. As such, he had cultivated the friendship of one Captain Girardi of the Italian military police in Rome, to whom he now expressed his outrage at the way in which 'honest French citizens' were being treated in Rome. Girardi suggested that such French citizens might address themselves to his own superior, General Presti, who was a man of considerable influence in the city. Schwamm and Father Benoît, who by now had learned that audacity was almost as good as authenticity, thereupon composed a letter to the general, protesting with great indignation the indignities to which French citizens were being subjected, and concluding by soliciting the general's help in the most ingratiating terms. The letter, on the stationery of the DELASEM committee and signed by Father Benoît, Executive Director, was then sent by messenger to the general's headquarters. General Presti replied immediately that he would see what he could do, and he requested the outraged Executive Director of the committee to be patient for a few days while he made 'inquiries.' It turned out that not much patience was necessary. The very next day, the police informed Father Benoît that, if he would send his friends to the bureau, residency permits would be forthcoming for them. In a very short time, all of Rome's Jews who were under the protection of DELASEM, now become the Committee for Refugee Assistance (provisional), were provided with residency permits.

It was necessary, of course, to continue these procedures for the benefit of new arrivals, of whom there were many every day of the week. Sometimes, however, such methods were not quick enough to avoid near disaster. On one occasion, a newly arrived French Jew had the misfortune to be picked up in a raid before he had had the opportunity to provide himself with the proper identification. Father Benoît was notified that he was being held at the Mussolini Barracks—an ominous sign. Schwamm, in his new *persona* of Bernard Lioré, volunteered to go to the prison and 'see what could be done.' Now, Stéphane Schwamm was a man of intelligence and culture, gifted, moreover, with a great talent for histrionics. In addition, in preparing for his role in life as Bernard Lioré, he had had the foresight to provide himself with a 'position'—as a Deputy Representative of the French Red Cross—and with credentials to match. It was as such that he presented himself, impeccably dressed and groomed, to the Commandant of the Mussolini Barracks. After showing his credentials —briefly, to be sure—the pseudo Lioré transfixed the commandant with that haughty glare that Frenchmen reserve for use on foreigners. 'We have learned that you are holding—by error, to be sure—a French citizen. Unless the man is released in my custody immediately, we will be obliged to take up the matter at a higher level.'

The commandant, though visibly impressed, protested that he was in no position to release a prisoner without orders from his superiors. Schwamm/Lioré, meticulously polishing the monocle that was part of his 'costume' (as he put it), spoke softly and vaguely of such things as 'war crimes' and the inevitable Allied liberation of Rome; and the commandant's protests grew weaker apace and less frequent. Fifteen minutes later, Schwamm and the former prisoner walked away from the Mussolini Barracks, leaving behind them a thoroughly relieved commandant. Needless to say, the freed man disappeared the very next day and was replaced by a French citizen with all his papers in order.

Stéphane Schwamm, for all his talent, eventually was arrested and sent to a concentration camp in Germany. The cause of this disaster, however, was not the fact that he was a Jew, but that he pretended to be an official of the Red Cross. One day he had intervened in the streets of Rome when the police were about to arrest a man who had no papers. Flourishing his Red Cross credentials, he claimed that the man was a French citizen and that he, as an official of the French branch of his organization, would accept the responsibility for him. The police, however, were simple 'cops on the beat,' too unsophisticated to be impressed by foreign credentials. They refused to hand over the man, and, when Schwamm persisted, they arrested him as well and took him to the local precinct. There, a fatal call to the Red Cross ended Schwamm's masquerade, and he stood, unmasked, as simple Bernard Lioré, French citizen, legal resident of Rome, and possessor of forged Red Cross identification. He was tried and convicted and, as punishment, was sent as a slave labourer to a camp in Silesia. That, however, was not the end of the story, or of Schwamm's career as a master forger. When his camp was liberated by the Russians in January 1945, Schwamm by then was so well established as Bernard Lioré that he had no way to prove his true identity. For the remainder of the war, he wandered about eastern Germany and Poland, going from one military governor to another and attempting to prove that he was Stéphane Schwamm, a French Jew, and to obtain papers in that name. He was always received courteously, and the governors always shook their heads, first in puzzlement and finally in refusal. This Kafkaesque nightmare ended only when Schwamm, in desperation, forged papers transforming him from Bernard Lioré back to Stéphane Schwamm. Eventually, in Budapest, he found friends to testify to his identity, and his papers were legalized.

Not all of Father Benoît's protégés were by any means as sophisticated as Schwamm in their use of forged papers, and some of the Jewish refugees who presented themselves at the Via Sicilia convent were so innocent and unworldly as to make it difficult to help them. In one such case, the refugee had been sent to Charrier's office for a ration card. He returned shortly afterward, and told Father Benoît that he had been refused a card, and in fact had been thrown out of the office. Father Benoît was aghast; Charrier had always been extremely co-operative, and it was difficult to understand what had happened. So, he went to see Charrier. The official was in a dark mood. 'Really, Father, I must insist that you tell your friends to be more discreet when they come here. Let me tell you what happened.'

The refugee had presented himself at Charrier's office as required, but when Charrier began, as he always did, to question the man about his nationality and his papers, he had replied in a voice loud enough to be heard throughout the entire building that 'these papers are not my real ones, you see. I am Jewish, not French. These are just documents that Father Benoît forged for me so that I could get a ration card. . . .' As heads began to turn in their direction, Charrier did the only thing that he could: he had the man ejected. 'By all means, Father,' he said, 'send the man back in a few days. But for heaven's sake tell him to play the game, will you?'

Not all of Father Benoît's problems were so easily solved. As the Allies approached closer and closer to Rome, the Gestapo became desperate and made every effort to put a stop to the priest's activities. On one occasion, a Franciscan convent that served as a clothing depot was raided. When no evidence of any wrongdoing was found—the sisters claimed that the large supply of men's clothing was for distribution among the poor, as part of their charitable work—the nuns were questioned at length, and not gently, about Father Benoît. Shortly afterward, an agent of DELASEM who was employed in the office of General Kappler, the Gestapo commandant, reported that the general had on his desk a warrant for the priest's arrest. Under the circumstances, it was decided to hold the next committee meeting at the office of a lawyer who was associated with DELASEM. The Gestapo learned of this, and in the middle of the meeting a telephone call was received to the effect that 'the Gestapo is on its way there.' Father Benoît and his associates escaped by a hair's breadth by leaving through a back door and scaling a stone wall just as the Gestapo was coming in through the front.

Not all his vexations, however, came from the Gestapo. He often received anonymous threatening letters, which he usually disregarded as the work of cranks. One such letter arrived that could not be ignored, as it went into great detail concerning the names of DELASEM workers and the location of distribution centres. It ended by demanding a payment of twenty thousand *lire* in exchange for the writer's silence. The money was to be delivered in the following week to a street corner near the Porta Pia; otherwise, the letter writer's information would be turned over to the Gestapo. The dilemma was deliberated by the committee, and it was concluded that the only solution was to 'convince' the extortionist, in one way or another, that DELASEM was not an easy mark. To have paid the money would only have invited similar attempts at blackmail later. On the appointed day, therefore, Brigadier General DeMarco, a new member of the DELASEM committee, went to the corner near the Porta Pia carrying the letter in his hand as instructed. He was followed closely by a group of tough-looking DELASEM workers. The woman, however—General DeMarco felt sure it was a woman—did not appear, or at least did not make herself known. Probably she had sensed a trap and decided that it was not worth it for a mere twenty thousand *lire*.

Such harassments, added to the constant threat of arrest, did not make life easy for DELASEM, but the organization continued its work without interruption until June 1944. On the fourth day of that month, the Allies entered Rome, and the Germans fled toward the north. And on that day it seemed that every one of Rome's million and a half people were in the streets, dancing and singing and welcoming the American troops. Shops were closed, the churches were full, bells rang, *Te Deums* were sung by the dozen.

For the first time in several years, Rome's Jews could walk the streets freely, without fear of arrest. The synagogues were immediately opened, and the people thanked God, once again, for their deliverance from the hands of the Gentiles. Their joy, however, was not undiluted. They were free again, it was true. But there was hardly a Jew on that day who had not lost a wife, a brother, a father or mother, to the holocaust. And in the synagogues, prayers of thanksgiving alternated with the mournful chants for the dead.

On the day on which the Allies entered Rome, the Committee for Refugee Assistance (provisional) breathed its last. Its work was done, and it expired willingly. It was replaced by a newly constituted DELASEM, whose work of relief and repatriation was now to begin in earnest. As DELASEM emerged from the cellars of the Capuchin convent into the new day, however, its president, Father Benoît, felt that it was now time to resign his post in favour of a Jewish president. His predecessor, Settimo Sorani, was elected once more, and Father Benoît was named honorary president for life.

The next few months were occupied with celebrations and with the details of the return to normal life. Among those celebrations were several in honour of Father

Benoît. One such meeting at Rome's chief synagogue, on the Lungotevere, was described by Father Benoît:

'I was accompanied by Father Calisto, representing the superior-general, and by Father Baudain and Father Archangel, who had been my collaborators for so long. And, of course, at my side was good Brother Basil, the porter, everyone's favourite because of his patience, kindness, and ingenuity.

'The meeting opened with the reading of a letter of thanks to my superior-general for his co-operation during our entire operation. Then, I was presented with the gift of a Bible inscribed with the signatures of all of my friends. . . . Next, a fine speech was read by M. Outzekhowsky, parts of which are worth reproducing:

> In the names of all those who are present, I take great pleasure in expressing to Father Marie-Benoît, and to the priests of his community, our most sincere and heartfelt gratitude for all that has been done for us by them at the risk of their lives.
>
> Who of us will ever be able to forget how, on that first miserable day in the orphanage, Father Benoît was already on hand to comfort us?
>
> It is in your honour, Father Benoît, our dear honorary president, that we have organized this celebration. It is a modest one, but for us it is full of meaning. We wish to give you a prize. We all know that there are all sorts of prizes in the world, but for you there is only one that is fitting, the greatest of them all, the prize for goodness and humanity. For you, Father Benoît, and your confreres; you all deserve the thanks of mankind.

This prize is, appropriately enough, a Bible. May this book keep us all from every evil. May it continue to enlighten us in all things for the good of humanity, in our love for all our brothers, and in all our actions.

My friends, let us rise. Let us turn our eyes to Father Benoît and to his brethren. For us, these men are the personification of goodness, of love, of humanity. Let us thank them.'

Father Benoît spoke last. He told of the great joy that he felt that the people of Israel were that day free in Rome, and that tomorrow they would be free throughout the world. 'Yet,' he said, 'it is a joy not unalloyed by sorrow and sadness. As we celebrate our liberation, we mourn our dead and we cry for those who must yet die before peace is finally re-established on earth. In the midst of our joy, let us remember, and let us pray for, those two thousand of our brothers who were taken from this city to a foreign land. They are not yet free. . . .'

'It is also a day of sadness because we will soon be returning each to his own people and to his own country. The parting of friends is not a happy thing; yet, we must rejoice and thank God that he has blessed us with so many dear friends. . . .

'Before parting, my good friends, let us resolve to accomplish a heroic act together. Let us promise ourselves to keep in mind always, and to live by that double commandment of the Mosaic law: You must love Yahweh, your God; and you must love your neighbour as yourself. Thus, we will remain always bound together in our hearts.'

Epilogue

ALMOST a quarter of a century has passed since Father Benoît's adventures in the Via Sicilia. Today, he is Father Superior of the Capuchin convent in Paris, an excellent administrator and teacher whose eyes still twinkle and whom responsibility has not deprived of his sense of humour. Occasionally, an event occurs that serves to remind the young clerics of the convent that their formidable superior once, many years ago, was an expert forger of documents, a fugitive from justice, and the head of Roman Jewry's most effective relief agency. He has been decorated by the French government for his activities in the resistance movement of that country, and he has been publicly honoured by the Government of Israel for his heroism in the rescue of Jews in France and Italy. The Italian government, too, has given public recognition to his work, and the words of Italy's President on that occasion in 1955, when he conferred a special gold medal of recognition on Father Benoît, serve admirably to sum up the sentiments of everyone, Jew and Gentile alike, who benefited from the Capuchin priest's belief that all men were indeed his brothers:

> Noteworthy indeed were his achievements, and without parallel was the work of rescue that he performed. An imposing example to all men, he worked with unfaltering courage and firm purpose, risking his life over and over again in order to help those who were in need of a friend. His accomplishments are worthy

of everlasting memory and eternal recognition.

Reports of Father Benoît's courage, and tales of his adventures, crossed the Atlantic, and he was praised and honoured by Jew and Gentile. One of his admirers was President Lyndon B. Johnson, who regarded Father Benoît as a model of the virtues that Americans should strive to cultivate:

> The heroic and fabulous feats of Father Marie-Benoît in rescuing Jews from the Gestapo during the Nazi occupation of Rome should inspire us in the United States to protect and respect the civil rights of all people, regardless of how they may differ from us in race, colour, or creed. Father Benoît saw the human dignity in the persecuted Jews and repeatedly risked his life to rescue them from the Gestapo and the incineration camps awaiting them. He blazed a trail for all of us to follow in protecting the civil and human rights of our fellow citizens and in thus respecting their dignity as fellow human beings.

Father Benoît accepts such tributes modestly, even unwillingly. There is, however, one token of recognition of which he is inordinately proud. It is the manuscript copy of a canticle sung by the Jewish children of Rome whom he had protected from the Nazis. The occasion was the testimonial meeting at the Lungotevere synagogue, and the canticle was composed for that gathering. The undoubted sincerity of the words, and the fervour with which they were sung, as Father Benoît testifies, supplied whatever was lacking in poetic quality:

> *To our dear Father Marie-Benoît,*
> *For having saved our own lives*

And those of thousands of others,
Long live Père Marie-Benoît!

The brave priest who saved us,
The one who gave us courage,
The one who protected us.
Food he found, and clothing,
And shelter for the children.
Long live Père Marie-Benoît!

For us he would have died,
For us he worked night and day,
Moved by a great love of God
To care for His unhappy children.
Long live Père Marie-Benoît!

He is our saviour,
He is our liberator,
Let us rejoice and be glad,
And pray to God for him.
Long live Père Marie-Benoît!

Father, you have reason to be proud
Of the thousands whom you saved.
We do our best to show our thanks,
But your reward must come from God.
Long live Père Marie-Benoît!

To our children we shall tell tales
Of this great priest, this great hero
Who fought for us so mightily,
And by his love saved us all.
To us, you have been,
And always you will remain,
Our most beloved father.